Lotus® 1-2-3® *Release 2.2*
Simplified User Guide

Richard Maran

Create and Sort a Database and
Graphing Chapters by Lynne Hoppen

Hypergraphics Inc.
Mississauga, Ontario, Canada

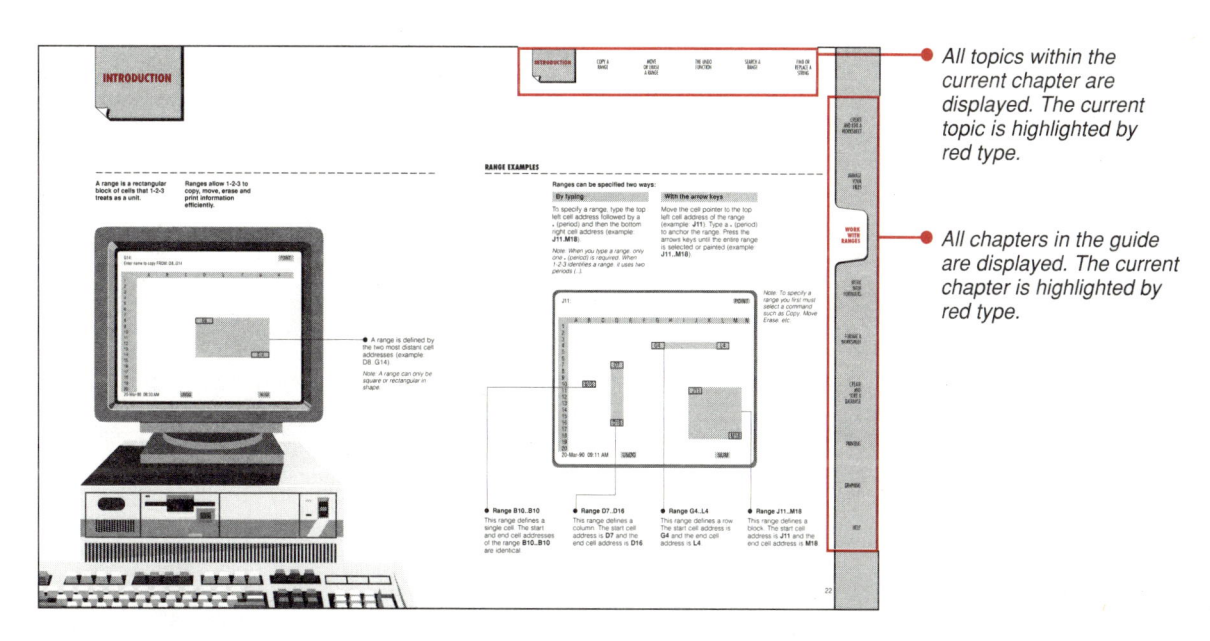

- All topics within the current chapter are displayed. The current topic is highlighted by red type.

- All chapters in the guide are displayed. The current chapter is highlighted by red type.

HOW TO USE THIS GUIDE

The table of contents is graphically represented on every right facing page. Quickly access the information you require by:

Finding the Chapter
While flipping through the pages of the guide, scan the right hand side of the page to locate the chapter you want.

Finding the Topic within the Chapter
Once you are within the desired chapter, scan the top right hand side of the pages to locate the topic you want. Flip to that highlighted page.

Lotus® 1-2-3® Release 2.2
Simplified User Guide

Copyright ©   Hypergraphics Inc. 1990
5755 Coopers Avenue
Mississauga, Ontario
Canada
L4Z 1R9

Published 1990. Second printing 1991

Canadian Cataloguing in Publication Data

Maran, Richard
Lotus 1-2-3, release 2.2 : simplified
user guide : beginner to intermediate

ISBN 0-9694290-1-0

1. Lotus 1-2-3 (Computer program).
2. Business – Data processing.
3. Electronic spreadsheets.
I. Hoppen, Lynne.   II. Title.

HF5548.4.L67M37 1990   005.369   C90-093890-0

All rights reserved. No part of this publication may be used, reproduced or transmitted, in any form or by any means, electronic, mechanical, photocopying, recording or otherwise, or stored in any retrieval system of any nature, without the prior written permission of the copyright holder, application for which shall be made to Hypergraphics Inc., 5755 Coopers Avenue, Mississauga, Ontario, Canada, L4Z 1R9.

This publication is sold with the understanding that neither Hypergraphics Inc., nor its dealers or distributors, warrants the contents of the publication, either expressly or impliedly, and, without limiting the generality of the foregoing, no warranty either express or implied is made regarding this publication's quality, performance, salability, capacity, suitability or fitness with respect to any specific or general function, purpose or application. Neither Hypergraphics Inc., nor its dealers or distributors shall be liable to the purchaser or any other person or entity in any shape, manner or form whatsoever regarding liability, loss or damage caused or alleged to be caused directly or indirectly by this publication.

Wholesale distribution:

Firefly Books Ltd.
250 Sparks Avenue
Willowdale, Ontario
Canada
M2H 2S4

Acknowledgements

A special thanks to Debbie Johnston of the Canadian Imperial Bank of Commerce for her expert guidance on content and technical accuracy. Also, to Lionel Koffler of Firefly Books for his contribution on visual style and format.

To the dedicated staff at Hypergraphics Inc. and HyperImage Inc., including Monica DeVries, Lynne Hoppen, Jim C. Leung, Robert Maran, Elizabeth Seeto, and Donna Williams for their technical support.

And finally to Maxine Maran for providing the organizational skill to keep the project under control.

Trademark Acknowledgements

Lotus and 1-2-3 are registered trademarks of Lotus Development Corporation.

IBM is a registered trademark of International Business Machines Corporation.

Xerox is a registered trademark of Xerox Corporation.

HP is a registered trademark of Hewlett Packard Corporation.

Cover Design:
Erich Volk

Art Direction:
Elizabeth Seeto

Production:
Jim C. Leung

Linotronic L-300 Output:
HyperImage Inc.

Table of Contents

CREATE AND EDIT A WORKSHEET
Start 1-2-3 2
Worksheet Introduction 4
Worksheet Navigation 6
Select Commands 8
Enter Labels 10
Enter Values 12

MANAGE YOUR FILES
Directories 14
Change the Default Directory 16
Display the Filename 17
Save a Worksheet 18
Retrieve a Worksheet 20
Erase a Worksheet 20

WORK WITH RANGES
Introduction 22
Copy a Range 24
Move or Erase a Range 28
The Undo Function 29
Search a Range 30
Find or Replace a String 31

WORK WITH FORMULAS
Introduction 32
Functions 34
Relative Cell References 36
Absolute Cell References 36

FORMAT A WORKSHEET
Change Cell Format 38
Change Column Width 40
Align Labels 42
Insert/Delete Rows or Columns 44

CREATE AND SORT A DATABASE
Introduction 46
Sort a Database 48

PRINTING
Select a Printer 50
Print Commands 51
Print a Report 52
Headers and Footers 54

GRAPHING
Define Type of Graph 56
Identify Data Ranges 57
Create Legend/Titles 58
View a Graph 59

HELP 60

INDEX 62

START 1-2-3

❶ To start 1-2-3® from DOS, type **CD\123** and press **Enter** to change the directory to 123.

❷ Type **LOTUS** and press **Enter**. The next screen appears.

or

Type **123** and press **Enter** to access the worksheet directly.

```
C> CD\123
C> LOTUS
```

For assistance on installing Lotus 1-2-3 on your hard drive, refer to the Lotus Reference Manual.

| START 1-2-3 | WORKSHEET INTRODUCTION | WORKSHEET NAVIGATION | SELECT COMMANDS | ENTER LABELS | ENTER VALUES |

● 1-2-3
This is the main worksheet program.

● PrintGraph
This utility is used to print graphs created in the worksheet.

● Translate
This utility transfers data between 1-2-3 and other programs.

● Install
This utility is used to customize the installation of 1-2-3 on your hard disk.

● Exit
Select Exit to return to DOS.

```
1-2-3   PrintGraph   Translate   Install   Exit
Use 1-2-3
```

                1-2-3 Access System
                Copyright 1986, 1989
              Lotus Development Corporation
                  All Rights Reserved
                      Release 2.2

The Access system lets you choose 1-2-3, PrintGraph, the Translate utility, and the Install program, from the menu at the top of this screen. If you're using a two-diskette system, the Access system may prompt you to change disks. Follow the instructions below to start a program.

○ Use → or ← to move the menu pointer (the highlighted rectangle at the top of the screen) to the program you want to use.

○ Press ENTER to start the program.

You can also start a program by typing the first character of its name.

Press HELP (F1) for more information.

The Access System allows you to move quickly between 1-2-3 and its utility programs.

To begin using a worksheet, type **1** (for 1-2-3).

CONVENTIONS

You can enter commands in either upper or lower case (example: /FR or /fr).

If key names are separated by a hyphen (-), press and hold down the first key before pressing the second key (example: Alt-F4).

If key names are separated by a space, press and release the first key before pressing the second key (example: End Home).

CREATE AND EDIT A WORKSHEET

MANAGE YOUR FILES

WORK WITH RANGES

WORK WITH FORMULAS

FORMAT A WORKSHEET

CREATE AND SORT A DATABASE

PRINTING

GRAPHING

HELP

3

WORKSHEET INTRODUCTION

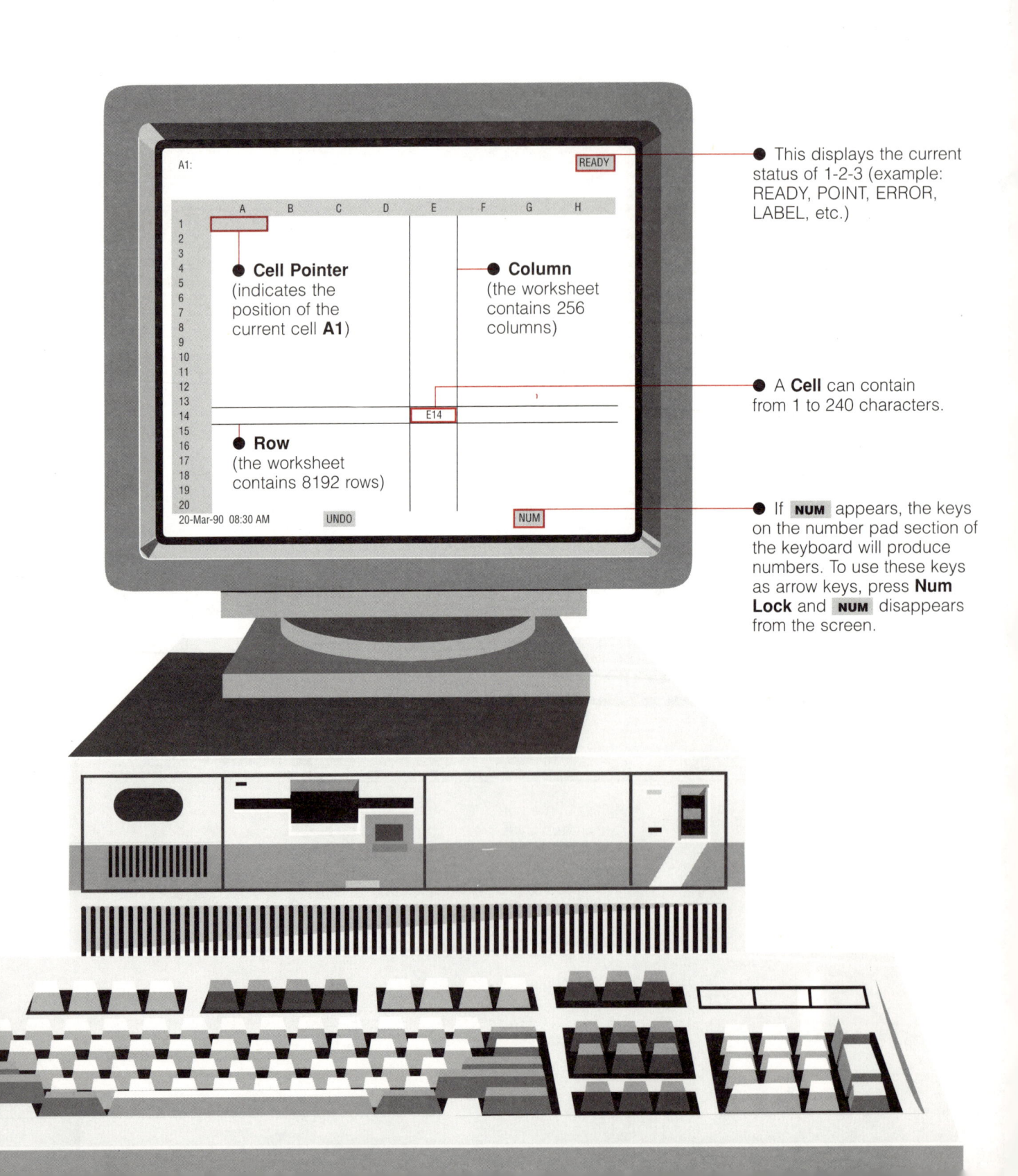

● This displays the current status of 1-2-3 (example: READY, POINT, ERROR, LABEL, etc.)

● **Cell Pointer** (indicates the position of the current cell **A1**)

● **Column** (the worksheet contains 256 columns)

● A **Cell** can contain from 1 to 240 characters.

● **Row** (the worksheet contains 8192 rows)

● If NUM appears, the keys on the number pad section of the keyboard will produce numbers. To use these keys as arrow keys, press **Num Lock** and NUM disappears from the screen.

START 1-2-3 | **WORKSHEET INTRODUCTION** | WORKSHEET NAVIGATION | SELECT COMMANDS | ENTER LABELS | ENTER VALUES

CREATE AND EDIT A WORKSHEET

● **Cell Address**

The Cell Address is the intersection of a Column and Row. In this example, the cell address is **C5**. This shows the current cursor position.

● **Cell Format**

The Cell Format defines how 1-2-3 displays a number in a cell. In this example, the Cell Format is **C**urrency with **0** decimal places.

● **Cell Width**

The Column Width is the number of characters that a column displays on screen. In this example, the Column Width is **12** characters.

● **Cell Entry**

The Cell Entry is the information entered into a cell. In this example, the Cell Entry is **1750000**.

```
C5:  (C0)  [W12]  1750000                                        READY
Worksheet  Range  Copy  Move  File  Print  Graph  Data  System  Add-In  Quit
Global  Insert  Delete  Column  Erase  Titles  Window  Status  Page  Learn
            A                    B              C              D
  1  CUSTOMER PROFILES
  2                         Account
  3  Company Name           Number       Assets         Liabilities
  4
  5  Systems Development Inc.  8563052    $1,750,000     $350,000
  6  Dalkin Properties Ltd.    7582652    $7,000,000   $1,750,000
  7  Simpson Manufacturing     8885773    $2,000,000     $950,000
  8  BAFCO Enterprises         4587602      $250,000       $4,000
  9  Solo Kitt Industries      7758290      $450,000      $17,000
 10  Steiner Pottery           7510205      $950,000     $350,000
 11  Newton Cleaners            572906      $857,000     $100,000
 12
 13
 14
 15
 16
 17
 18
 19
 20
 20-Mar-90  10:30 AM     UNDO
```

● **Main Menu**

This line contains all the Main commands of Lotus 1-2-3.

● **Submenu or Description of Command**

This line contains a list of Submenu commands that relate to the highlighted command in the Main menu (example: Worksheet).

Note: For certain commands in the Main menu, such as Copy, this line contains a description of the command.

MANAGE YOUR FILES

WORK WITH RANGES

WORK WITH FORMULAS

FORMAT A WORKSHEET

CREATE AND SORT A DATABASE

PRINTING

GRAPHING

HELP

WORKSHEET NAVIGATION

MOVE ONE CELL IN ANY DIRECTION

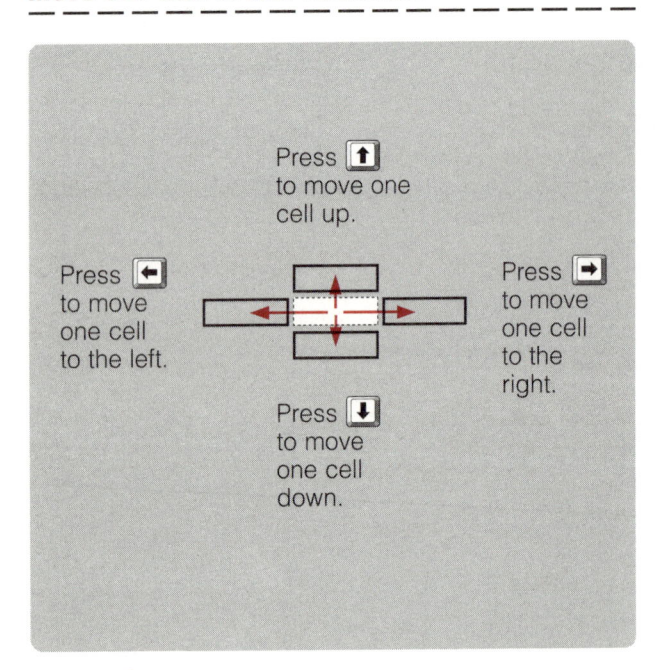

Press ⬆ to move one cell up.

Press ⬅ to move one cell to the left.

Press ➡ to move one cell to the right.

Press ⬇ to move one cell down.

MOVE TO A1

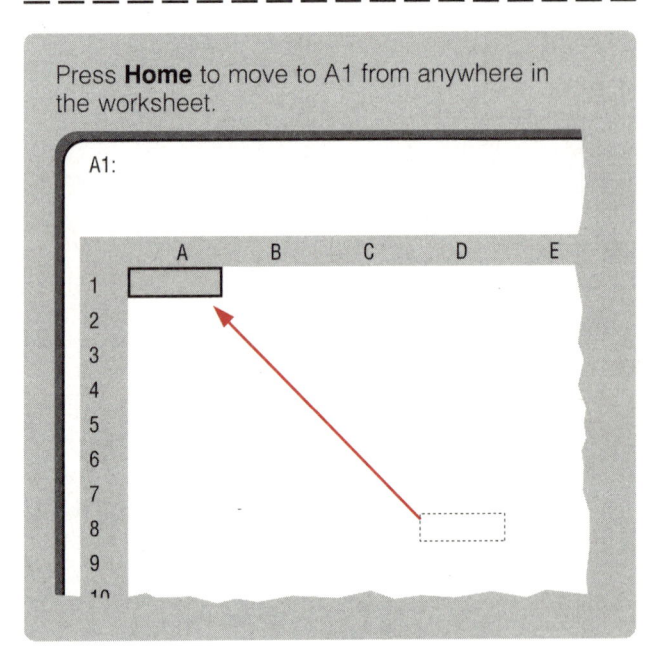

Press **Home** to move to A1 from anywhere in the worksheet.

MOVE ONE SCREEN RIGHT OR LEFT

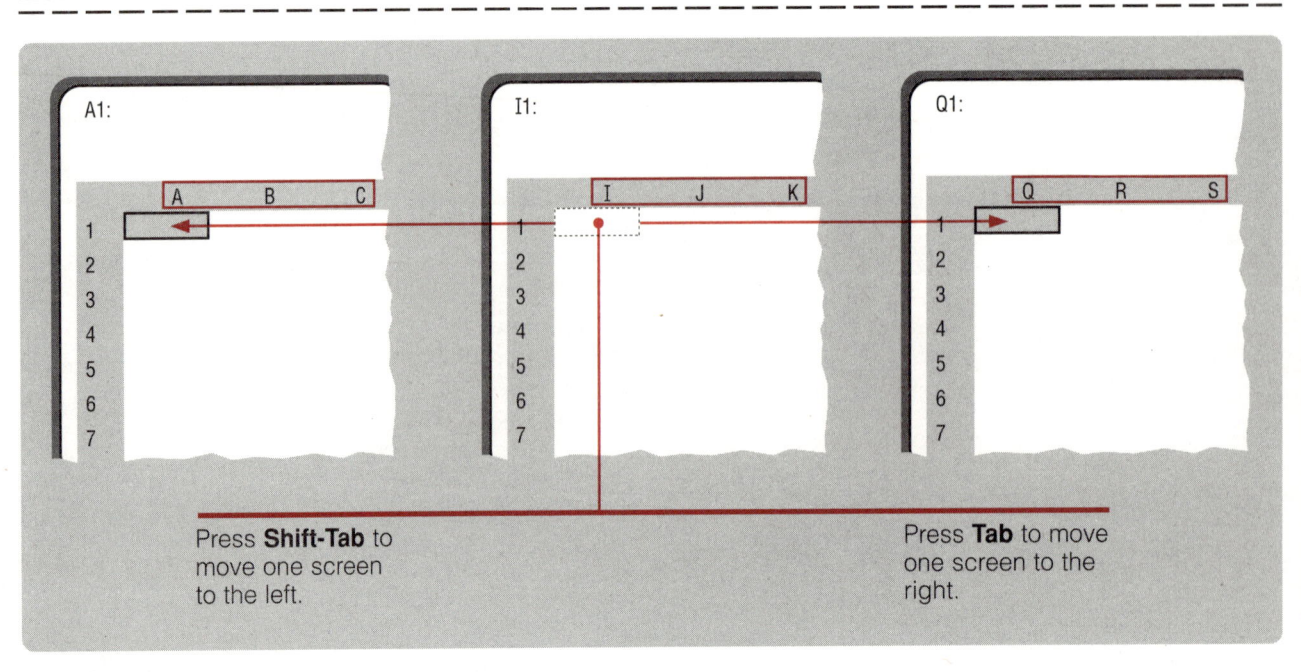

Press **Shift-Tab** to move one screen to the left.

Press **Tab** to move one screen to the right.

| START 1-2-3 | WORKSHEET INTRODUCTION | **WORKSHEET NAVIGATION** | SELECT COMMANDS | ENTER LABELS | ENTER VALUES |

MOVE ONE SCREEN UP OR DOWN

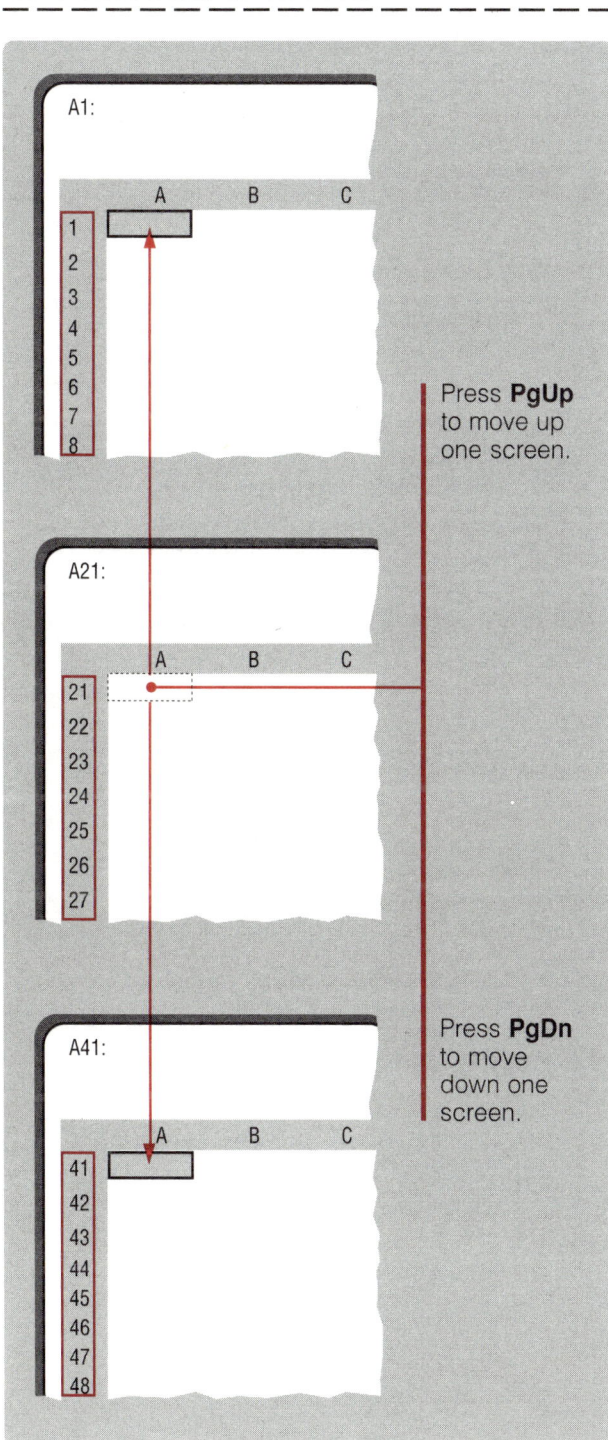

A1:

Press **PgUp** to move up one screen.

A21:

Press **PgDn** to move down one screen.

A41:

MOVE TO ANY CELL IN THE WORKSHEET

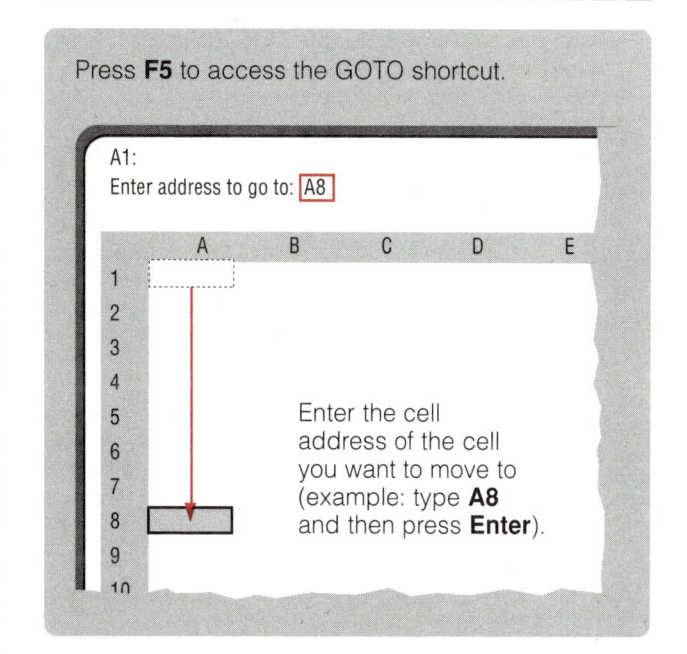

Press **F5** to access the GOTO shortcut.

A1:
Enter address to go to: A8

Enter the cell address of the cell you want to move to (example: type **A8** and then press **Enter**).

MOVE TO THE RIGHT EDGE OF THE WORKSHEET (COLUMN IV)

Press **End** →.

Note: These keys may have to be pressed more than once to get to the desired location.

MOVE TO THE BOTTOM EDGE OF THE WORKSHEET (ROW 8192)

Press **End** ↓.

Note: These keys may have to be pressed more than once to get to the desired location.

MOVE TO THE LOWER RIGHT CORNER OF DATA STORED IN THE WORKSHEET

Press **End Home**.

CREATE AND EDIT A WORKSHEET

MANAGE YOUR FILES

WORK WITH RANGES

WORK WITH FORMULAS

FORMAT A WORKSHEET

CREATE AND SORT A DATABASE

PRINTING

GRAPHING

HELP

7

SELECT COMMANDS

When 1-2-3 is in the READY mode, type **/** to activate the Main menu.

To select a command from any Lotus menu, press ⬅ or ➡ as many times as needed until the required command is highlighted. Then press **Enter**.

Note: To return to the READY mode press **Ctrl-Break**.

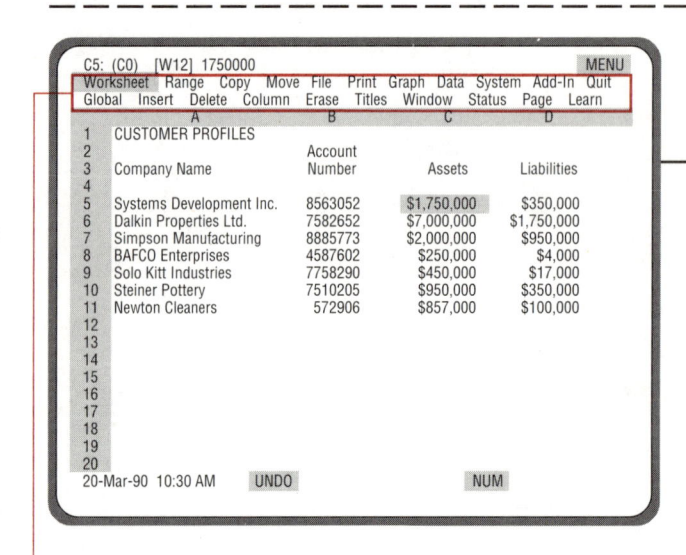

EXAMPLE: SELECT COMMANDS TO ERASE A WORKSHEET FROM THE SCREEN

```
C5: (C0)  [W12] 1750000                                        MENU
Worksheet Range Copy Move File Print Graph Data System Add-In Quit
Global Insert Delete Column Erase Titles Window Status Page Learn
          A              B            C            D
 1    CUSTOMER PROFILES
 2                         Account
 3    Company Name         Number     Assets       Liabilities
 4
 5    Systems Development Inc.  8563052   $1,750,000   $350,000
 6    Dalkin Properties Ltd.    7582652   $7,000,000   $1,750,000
 7    Simpson Manufacturing     8885773   $2,000,000   $950,000
 8    BAFCO Enterprises         4587602     $250,000     $4,000
 9    Solo Kitt Industries      7758290     $450,000    $17,000
10    Steiner Pottery           7510205     $950,000   $350,000
11    Newton Cleaners            572906     $857,000   $100,000
12
...
20
20-Mar-90 10:30 AM      UNDO              NUM
```

❶ Type **/** to activate the Main menu.

❷ To select Worksheet, press **Enter** and the next screen appears.

EXAMPLE: SELECT COMMANDS TO ERASE A WORKSHEET FROM THE SCREEN

SHORTCUT TO SELECT COMMANDS

Typing the first letters in a command sequence (example: **W**orksheet **E**rase **Y**es) eliminates the need to use the **Arrow** and **Enter** keys.

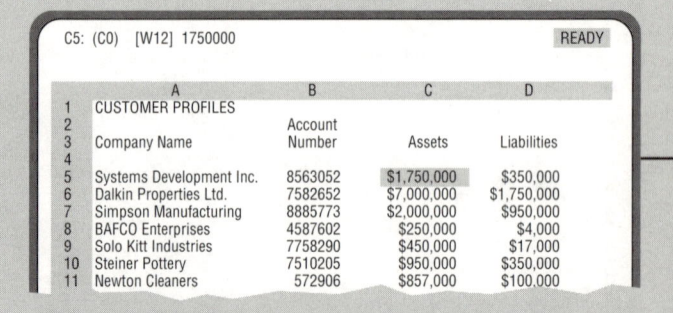

```
C5: (C0)  [W12] 1750000                                       READY

          A              B            C            D
 1    CUSTOMER PROFILES
 2                         Account
 3    Company Name         Number     Assets       Liabilities
 4
 5    Systems Development Inc.  8563052   $1,750,000   $350,000
 6    Dalkin Properties Ltd.    7582652   $7,000,000   $1,750,000
 7    Simpson Manufacturing     8885773   $2,000,000   $950,000
 8    BAFCO Enterprises         4587602     $250,000     $4,000
 9    Solo Kitt Industries      7758290     $450,000    $17,000
10    Steiner Pottery           7510205     $950,000   $350,000
11    Newton Cleaners            572906     $857,000   $100,000
```

❶ When 1-2-3 is in the READY mode, type **/WEY** and the next screen appears.

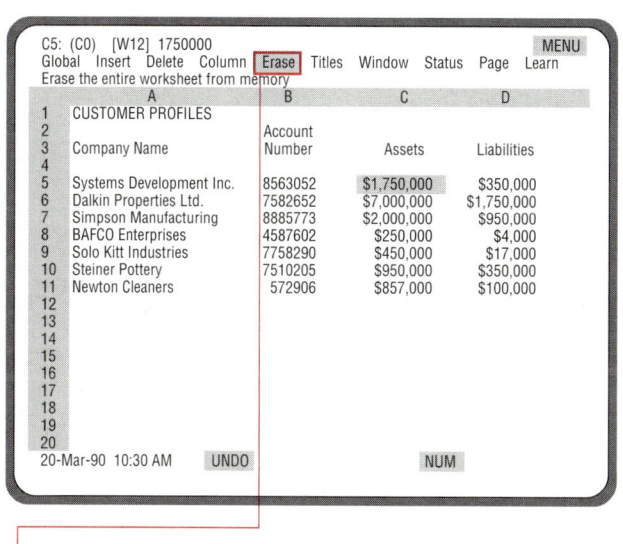

START | WORKSHEET | WORKSHEET | **SELECT COMMANDS** | ENTER | ENTER
1-2-3 | INTRODUCTION | NAVIGATION | | LABELS | VALUES

CREATE AND EDIT A WORKSHEET

MANAGE YOUR FILES

❸ Press ➡ four times to select Erase.

❹ Press **Enter** and the next screen appears.

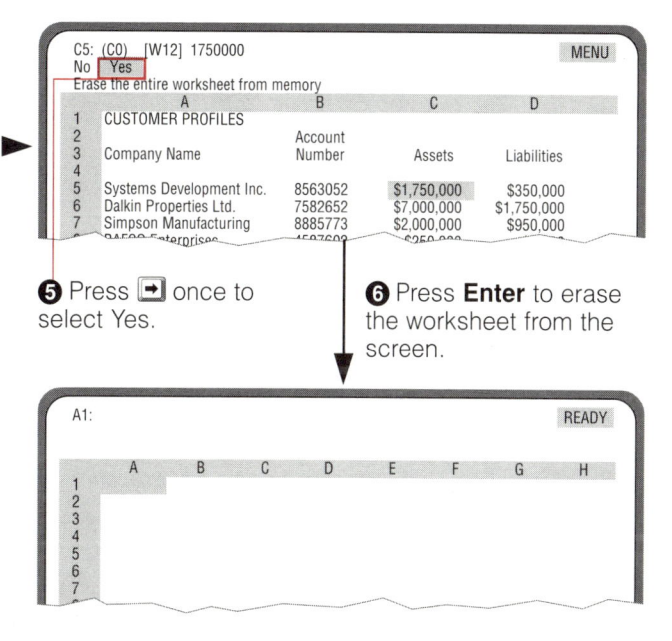

❺ Press ➡ once to select Yes.

❻ Press **Enter** to erase the worksheet from the screen.

WORK WITH RANGES

● The worksheet is erased.

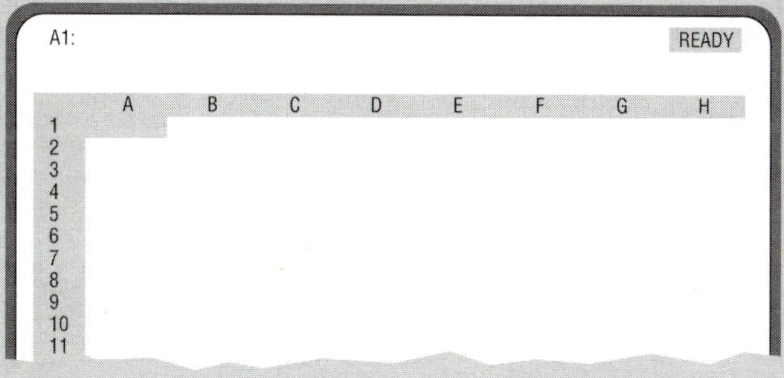

WORK WITH FORMULAS

FORMAT A WORKSHEET

CREATE AND SORT A DATABASE

● The worksheet is erased.

To back up through the menu system one step at a time

Press **Esc** as many times as required.

PRINTING

GRAPHING

To immediately return to the READY mode

Press **Ctrl-Break**.

HELP

9

ENTER LABELS

RULES FOR ENTERING LABELS

- Labels contain text. The text can include letters and/or numbers. The numbers, however, cannot be used in a calculation.
- The word LABEL appears in the top right corner of the screen when a label is typed.
- The label appears at the left edge of a cell unless otherwise specified by a label prefix.
- A label may not begin with a number unless preceded by a label prefix.
- A label can contain spaces and commas.

Long Labels

- If a label is too long to fit into a cell, its text spills over into adjacent cell(s), if they are empty.
- If the adjacent cell already contains data, 1-2-3 displays as much of the label as it can. To display the entire label, the column must be widened.

ENTER LABELS

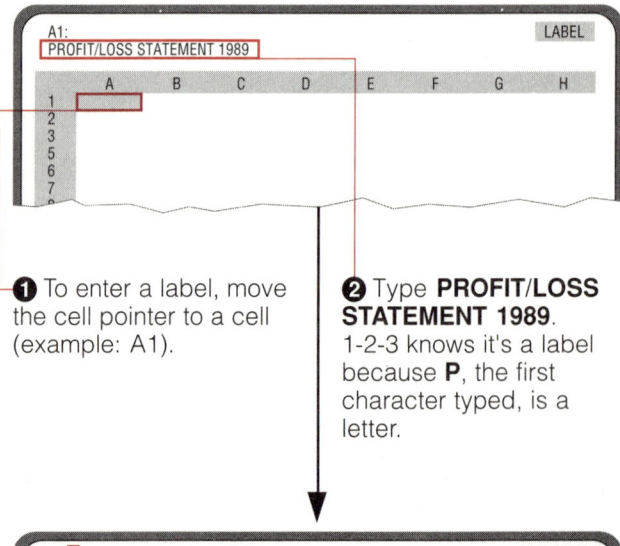

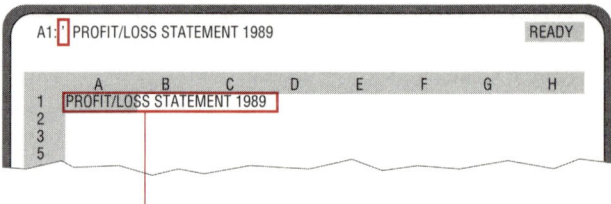

❶ To enter a label, move the cell pointer to a cell (example: A1).

❷ Type **PROFIT/LOSS STATEMENT 1989**. 1-2-3 knows it's a label because **P**, the first character typed, is a letter.

❸ Press **Enter** to place the label in cell A1.

1-2-3 automatically includes the label prefix ' (apostrophe) when a letter is the first character typed.

Note: The label prefix ' is the default setting. It aligns the label to the left edge of the cell.

Labels that start with numbers

If the first character in a label is a number, type a label prefix before the first character to identify it as a label (example: '1990 BUDGET).

Label prefixes

'   Placing ' before a label aligns it to the left side of the cell.

"   Placing " before a label aligns it to the right side of the cell.

^   Placing ^ before a label centers it in the cell.

\   Placing \ before a character (such as a dash) fills the cell with that character.

| START 1-2-3 | WORKSHEET INTRODUCTION | WORKSHEET NAVIGATION | SELECT COMMANDS | **ENTER LABELS** | ENTER VALUES |

CREATE AND EDIT A WORKSHEET

CORRECT/EDIT LABELS BEFORE PRESSING ENTER

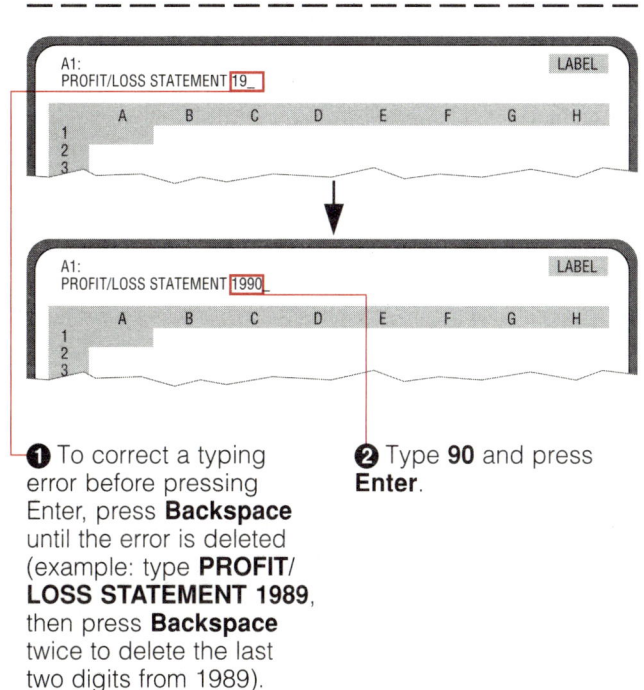

A1:
PROFIT/LOSS STATEMENT 19_   LABEL

↓

A1:
PROFIT/LOSS STATEMENT 1990_   LABEL

❶ To correct a typing error before pressing Enter, press **Backspace** until the error is deleted (example: type **PROFIT/LOSS STATEMENT 1989**, then press **Backspace** twice to delete the last two digits from 1989).

❷ Type **90** and press **Enter**.

CORRECT/EDIT LABELS AFTER PRESSING ENTER

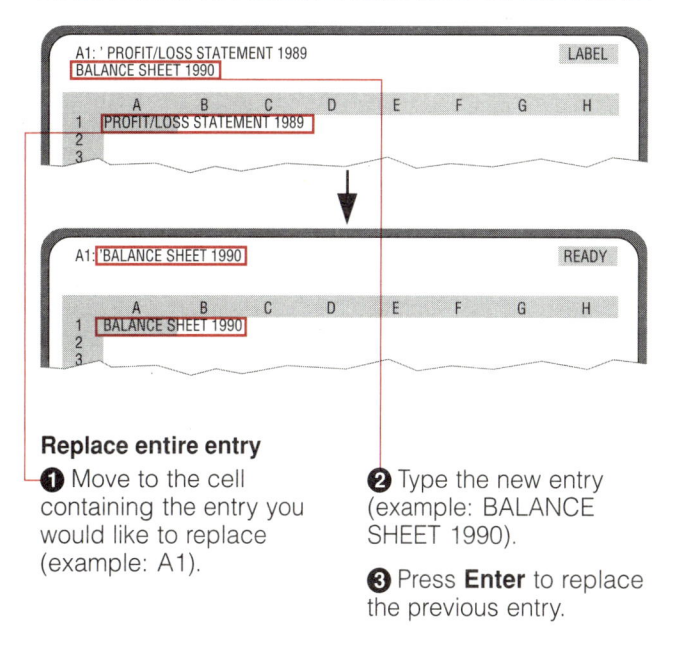

A1: ' PROFIT/LOSS STATEMENT 1989
BALANCE SHEET 1990   LABEL

    PROFIT/LOSS STATEMENT 1989

↓

A1: 'BALANCE SHEET 1990   READY

    BALANCE SHEET 1990

Replace entire entry

❶ Move to the cell containing the entry you would like to replace (example: A1).

❷ Type the new entry (example: BALANCE SHEET 1990).

❸ Press **Enter** to replace the previous entry.

Edit minor changes to entry

❶ Move to the cell containing the incorrect entry and press **F2** (the Edit key).

❷ Move the cursor to the point of change and type the correction. Refer to the table below.

❸ Press **Enter** to save the changes.

or

Press **Esc** to leave the Edit mode without saving the change.

Edit key descriptions	
Home	– Move to the beginning of the data.
End	– Move to the end of the data.
Tab	– Move 5 characters to the right each time Tab is pressed.
Shift-Tab	– Move 5 characters to the left each time Shift-Tab is pressed.
← or →	– Move one character in the direction of the arrow.
Delete	– Erase the character the cursor is on.
Backspace	– Erase the character to the left of the cursor.

MANAGE YOUR FILES

WORK WITH RANGES

WORK WITH FORMULAS

FORMAT A WORKSHEET

CREATE AND SORT A DATABASE

PRINTING

GRAPHING

HELP

11

ENTER VALUES

ENTER NUMBERS

To enter a number into the worksheet, use the arrow keys to position the cell pointer at the cell to be filled.

Type the number. If more data must be typed in other cells, use the arrow key(s) to move to the next cell to fill.

To keep the cell pointer in the cell after typing, press **Enter**.

ENTER A FORMULA

A formula must begin with a number or an operator + − (@ . $.

To enter a formula into the worksheet, use the arrow key(s) to position the cell pointer at the cell to contain the formula.

Type the formula into the cell and then press either **Enter** or an arrow key.

AUTOMATIC RECALCULATION

Cell addresses are normally used in formulas instead of numbers. Then, if the numbers in the cells change, the formula automatically recalculates the new result.

RULES FOR ENTERING VALUES

- A value is either a number or a formula. A formula is an entry that performs a calculation. The result of the calculation appears in the cell.
- The word VALUE appears in the top right corner of the screen when a value is typed.
- A value appears at the right edge of a cell. Its position cannot be changed.
- A value begins with a number (0 through 9), or operator + − (@ . $.
- A value cannot contain spaces or commas.
- A value can only contain one decimal point.

Long Values

- When a value is too long to fit in a cell, 1-2-3 tries to display it exponentially. If the exponential form is still too long, asterisks are displayed in the cell. To display the whole value, the column must be widened.

| START 1-2-3 | WORKSHEET INTRODUCTION | WORKSHEET NAVIGATION | SELECT COMMANDS | ENTER LABELS | **ENTER VALUES** |

CREATE AND EDIT A WORKSHEET

EXAMPLE:

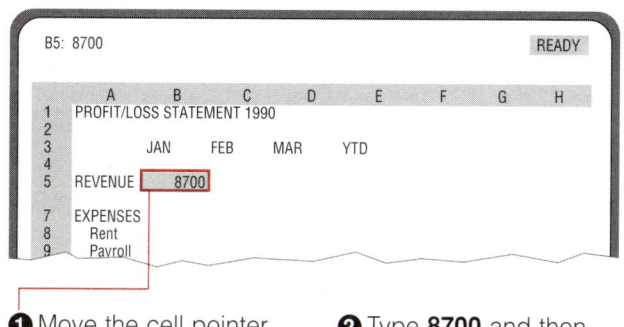

```
B5: 8700                                    READY
   A        B      C      D      E    F    G    H
1  PROFIT/LOSS STATEMENT 1990
2
3           JAN    FEB    MAR    YTD
4
5  REVENUE  8700
6
7  EXPENSES
8    Rent
9    Payroll
```

```
C5: 9100                                    READY
   A        B      C      D      E    F    G    H
1  PROFIT/LOSS STATEMENT 1990
2
3           JAN    FEB    MAR    YTD
4
5  REVENUE  8700  9100
6
7  EXPENSES
8    Rent
9    Payroll
```

❶ Move the cell pointer to B5.

❷ Type **8700** and then press ➡. This enters 8700 and moves the cell pointer to C5.

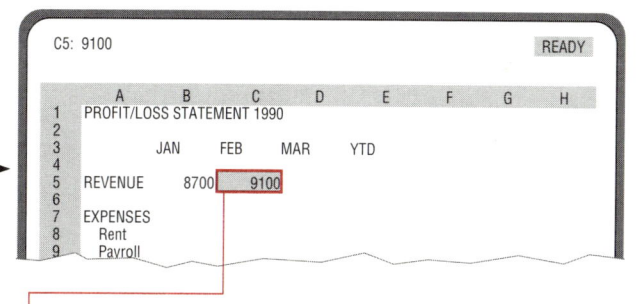

❸ Type **9100** and then press **Enter**. This enters 9100 and keeps the cell pointer in C5.

Note: If a cell already contains information, the old data is replaced by the new entry.

EXAMPLE:

```
E5: +B5+C5+D5                               READY
   A        B      C      D      E    F    G    H
1  PROFIT/LOSS STATEMENT 1990
2
3           JAN    FEB    MAR    YTD
4
5  REVENUE  8700  9100  9200
6
7  EXPENSES
8    Rent
9    Payroll
```

```
E5: +B5+C5+D5                               READY
   A        B      C      D      E    F    G    H
1  PROFIT/LOSS STATEMENT 1990
2
3           JAN    FEB    MAR    YTD
4
5  REVENUE  8700  9100  9200  27000
6
7  EXPENSES
8    Rent
9    Payroll
```

❶ Move the cell pointer to E5.

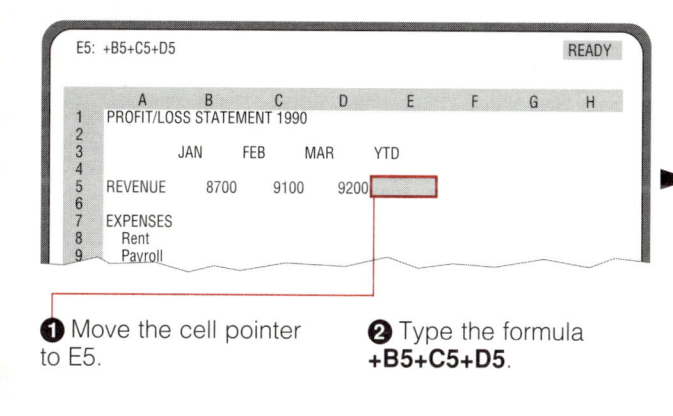

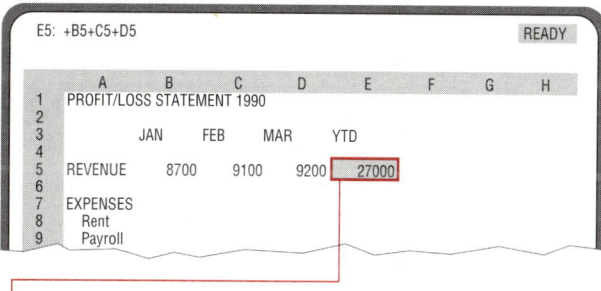

❷ Type the formula **+B5+C5+D5**.

❸ Press **Enter**. 1-2-3 adds +B5+C5+D5 and displays the sum in E5.

EXAMPLE:

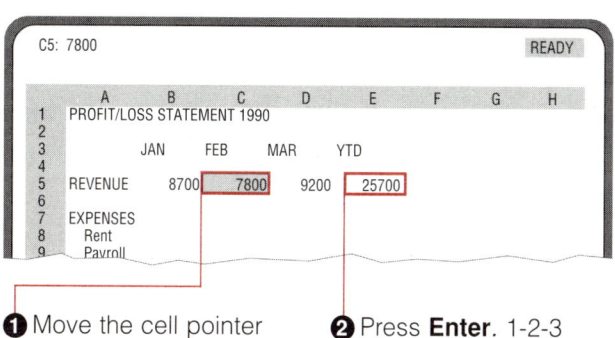

```
C5: 7800                                    READY
   A        B      C      D      E    F    G    H
1  PROFIT/LOSS STATEMENT 1990
2
3           JAN    FEB    MAR    YTD
4
5  REVENUE  8700  7800  9200  25700
6
7  EXPENSES
8    Rent
9    Payroll
```

❶ Move the cell pointer to C5 and type **7800** to replace 9100.

❷ Press **Enter**. 1-2-3 automatically recalculates E5 and displays 25700.

MANAGE YOUR FILES

WORK WITH RANGES

WORK WITH FORMULAS

FORMAT A WORKSHEET

CREATE AND SORT A DATABASE

PRINTING

GRAPHING

HELP

13

DIRECTORIES

DIRECTORY ORGANIZATION

This chart illustrates how a financial institution might organize their PC software and data files on a hard disk.

Each program (example: Lotus 1-2-3, WordPerfect) is located in a separate subdirectory, one level below the Root Directory.

Worksheets are stored in different subdirectories (example: POST01, POST02, POST03, POST04), which are one level below the 123DATA subdirectory.

Each POST subdirectory contains work done by a specific individual.

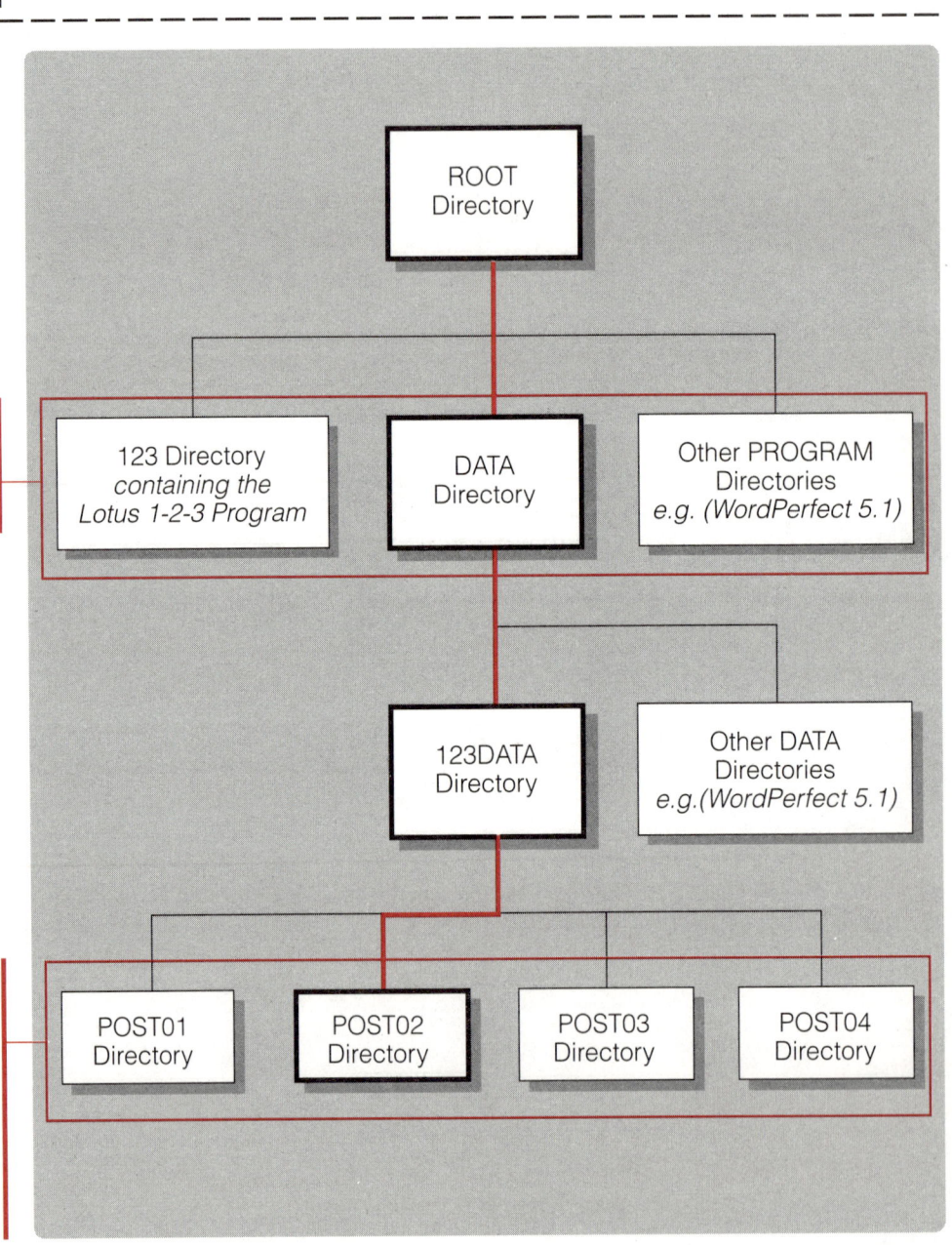

```
                    ROOT
                  Directory
                      |
        ┌─────────────┼─────────────┐
        |             |             |
   123 Directory    DATA      Other PROGRAM
   containing the  Directory    Directories
   Lotus 1-2-3                e.g. (WordPerfect 5.1)
   Program
                      |
                ┌─────┴─────┐
                |           |
             123DATA    Other DATA
            Directory   Directories
                       e.g.(WordPerfect 5.1)
                |
     ┌──────┬───┴───┬──────┐
     |      |       |      |
  POST01  POST02  POST03  POST04
 Directory Directory Directory Directory
```

The path from the *ROOT Directory* to the *POST02 Directory* is:

C:\DATA\123DATA\POST02

14

| DIRECTORIES | CHANGE THE DEFAULT DIRECTORY | DISPLAY THE FILENAME | SAVE A WORKSHEET | RETRIEVE A WORKSHEET | ERASE A WORKSHEET |

CREATE DIRECTORIES

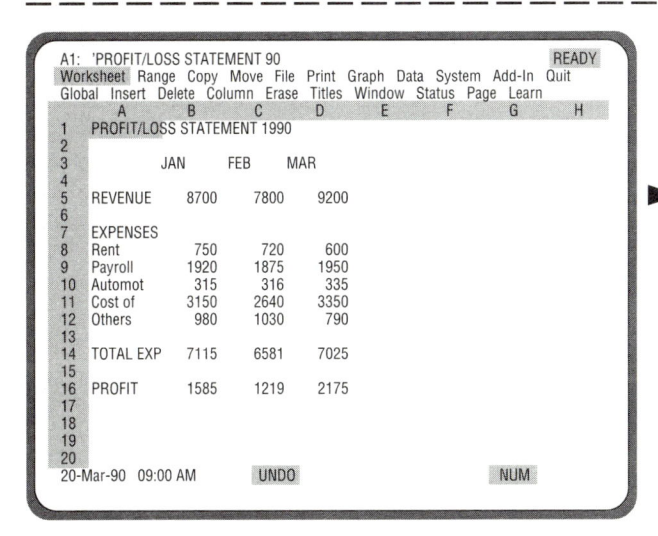

You can return to the operating system without ending the current 1-2-3 session.

❶ Type **/S** (for **S**ystem) and the next screen appears.

Create the DATA Directory

❷ Type **MD\DATA** (**MD** stands for **M**ake **D**irectory, and **\DATA** is the directory being created).

❸ Press **Enter**.

Create the 123DATA Directory

❹ Type **MD\DATA\123DATA**.

❺ Press **Enter**.

Create the POST02 Directory

❻ Type **MD\DATA\123DATA\POST02**.

❼ Press **Enter**.

❽ Create the POST01, POST03 and POST04 directories as per Steps **6** and **7**.

❾ To return to 1-2-3 type **EXIT** and then press **Enter**.

FILE NAMING RULES

ABCDE123 .WK1

- This part of the name can contain up to 8 characters.
- 1-2-3 automatically assigns a file extension of .WK1.

The following characters are allowed:
- The letters A to Z, upper or lower case
- The digits 0 through 9
- $ # & @ ! % ( ) - { } and ~

CREATE AND EDIT A WORKSHEET

MANAGE YOUR FILES

WORK WITH RANGES

WORK WITH FORMULAS

FORMAT A WORKSHEET

CREATE AND SORT A DATABASE

PRINTING

GRAPHING

HELP

15

CHANGE THE DEFAULT DIRECTORY

DISPLAY THE FILENAME

CHANGE THE DEFAULT DIRECTORY

```
A1:                                                    EDIT
  Enter default directory: C:\DATA\123DATA
              ┌──────── Default Settings ────────┐
  Printer:                    Directory: C:\DATA\123DATA
    Interface    Parallel 1
    Auto linefeed  No         Autoexecute macros:  Yes
    Margins
       Left 4  Right 76  Top 2 Bottom 2    International:
    Page length  66              Punctuation      A
    Wait         No                Decimal        Period
    Setup string                   Argument       Comma
    Name         XEROX 4045-50 Couri...  Thousands  Comma
                              Currency         Prefix: $
  Add-In:                     Date format (D4) A (MM/DD/YY)
    1                         Time format (D8) A (HH:MM:SS)
    2                         Negative         Parentheses
    3
    4                         Help access method: Removable
    5                         Clock display:    Standard
    6                         Undo:             Enabled
    7                         Beep:             Yes
    8

  20-Mar-90  09:27 AM                              NUM
```

```
A1:                                                    FILES
  Name of file to retrieve: C:\DATA\123DATA\*.wk?
  POST01\    POST02\    POST03\    POST04\
         A        B        C        D        E        F        G        H
   1
   2
   3
   4
   5
   6
   7
   8
   9
  10
  11
  12
  13
  14
  15
  16
  17
  18
  19
  20
  20-Mar-90  09:27 AM                              NUM
```

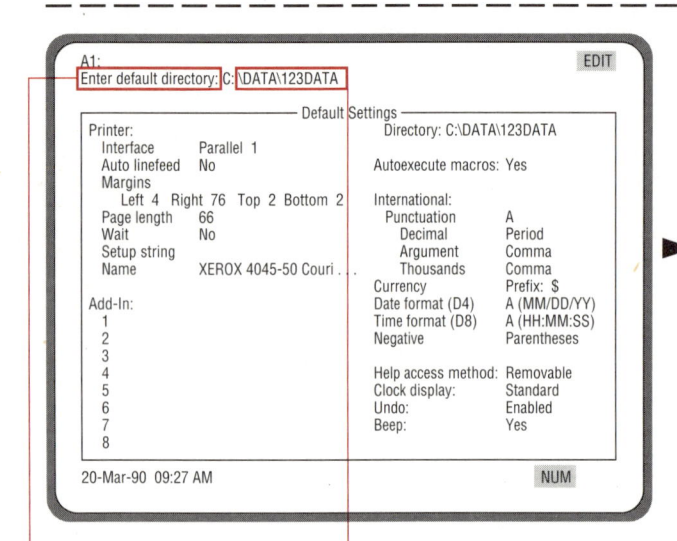

The directory C:\123 contains the 1-2-3 program files and is normally set up as the default directory.

Data files, however, are normally stored in and retrieved from other subdirectories (example: POST01, POST02, POST03 and POST04).

To change the default directory

❶ Type **/WGDD** (for **W**orksheet **G**lobal **D**efault **D**irectory) and the prompt above appears.

❷ Type the path to the work subdirectories set up earlier—POST01, POST02, POST03 and POST04 (example: **C:\DATA\123DATA**).

Note: Use Backspace Insert, Delete and the cursor keys to help type and edit the path name.

❸ Press **Enter**.

❹ To save this new default setting for future 1-2-3 sessions, type **UQ** (for **U**pdate **Q**uit). This also returns 1-2-3 to the READY mode.

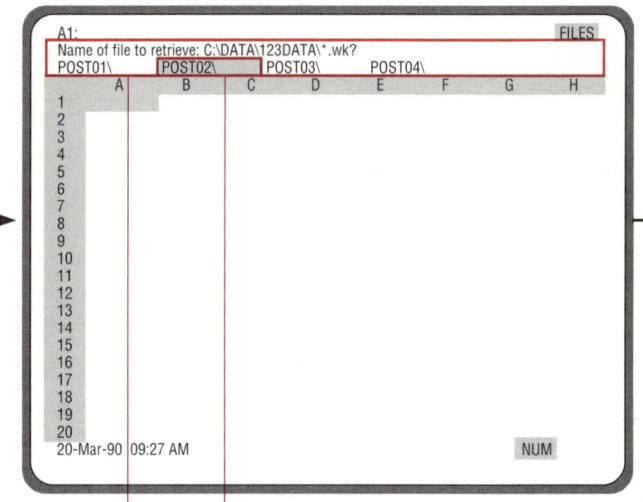

❺ Type **/FR** (for **F**ile **R**etrieve) and the prompt above appears.

The default directory setting of C:\DATA\123DATA brings up the subdirectories POST01, POST02, POST03 and POST04.

❻ Press ➡ once to highlight the POST02 subdirectory.

16

DIRECTORIES | **CHANGE THE DEFAULT DIRECTORY** | **DISPLAY THE FILENAME** | SAVE A WORKSHEET | RETRIEVE A WORKSHEET | ERASE A WORKSHEET

DISPLAY THE FILENAME

Display filename

Normally, the date and time appear in the bottom left corner of the screen.

❶ To display the filename instead of the date and time, type **/WGDOCF** (for **W**orksheet **G**lobal **D**efault **O**ther **C**lock **F**ilename).

❷ To return to the READY mode, type **Q** (for **Q**uit). Or, to save this setting for future 1-2-3 sessions, type **UQ** (for **U**pdate **Q**uit). This also returns 1-2-3 to the READY mode.

❼ Press **Enter** and the worksheets in the POST02 subdirectory are listed across the screen.

❽ Press ← or → to highlight the worksheet required and then press **Enter** to retrieve it.

or

Type the worksheet filename (example: PROFIT90) and then press **Enter** to retrieve it.

Note: There may be more files in the subdirectory than can be displayed across the screen. To see more filenames, keep pressing →.

Display date and time

❶ To display the date and time instead of the filename, type **/WGDOCC** (For **W**orksheet **G**lobal **D**efault **O**ther **C**lock **C**lock).

❷ To return to the READY mode, type **Q** (for **Q**uit). Or, to save this setting for future 1-2-3 sessions, type **UQ** (for **U**pdate **Q**uit). This also returns 1-2-3 to the READY mode.

CREATE AND EDIT A WORKSHEET

MANAGE YOUR FILES

WORK WITH RANGES

WORK WITH FORMULAS

FORMAT A WORKSHEET

CREATE AND SORT A DATABASE

PRINTING

GRAPHING

HELP

17

SAVE A WORKSHEET

SAVE A NEW WORKSHEET

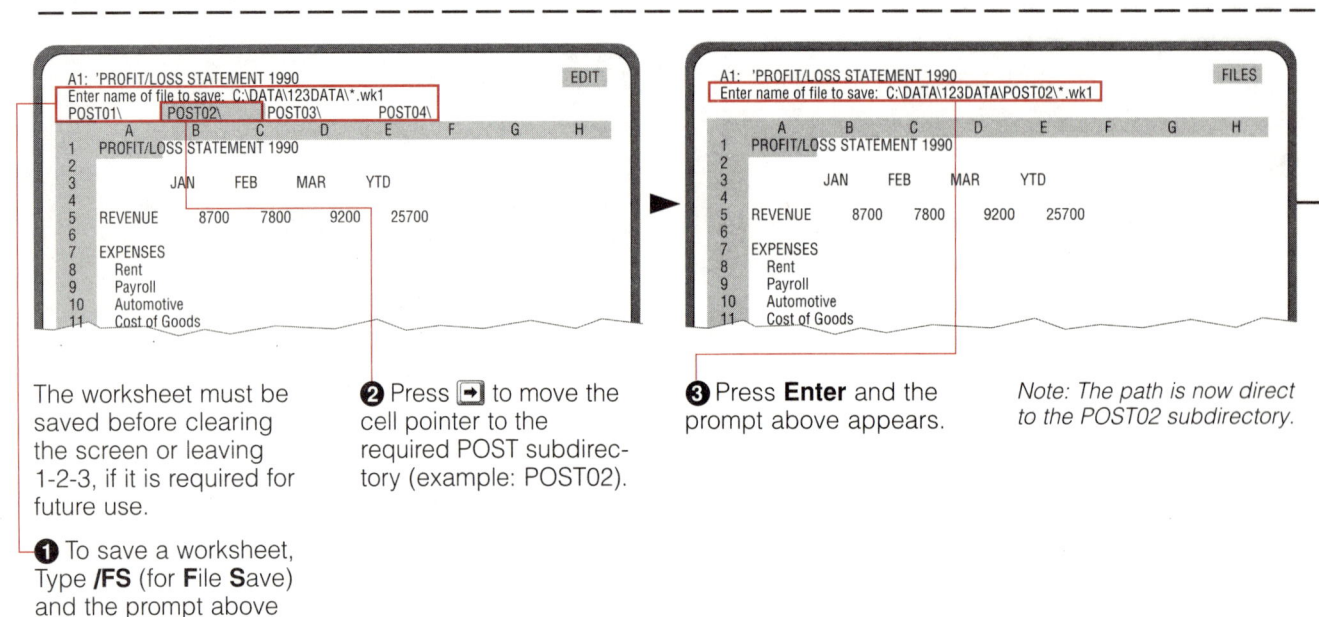

The worksheet must be saved before clearing the screen or leaving 1-2-3, if it is required for future use.

❶ To save a worksheet, Type **/FS** (for **F**ile **S**ave) and the prompt above appears.

❷ Press ➡ to move the cell pointer to the required POST subdirectory (example: POST02).

❸ Press **Enter** and the prompt above appears.

Note: The path is now direct to the POST02 subdirectory.

SAVE A REVISED WORKSHEET (to the current directory with the current filename)

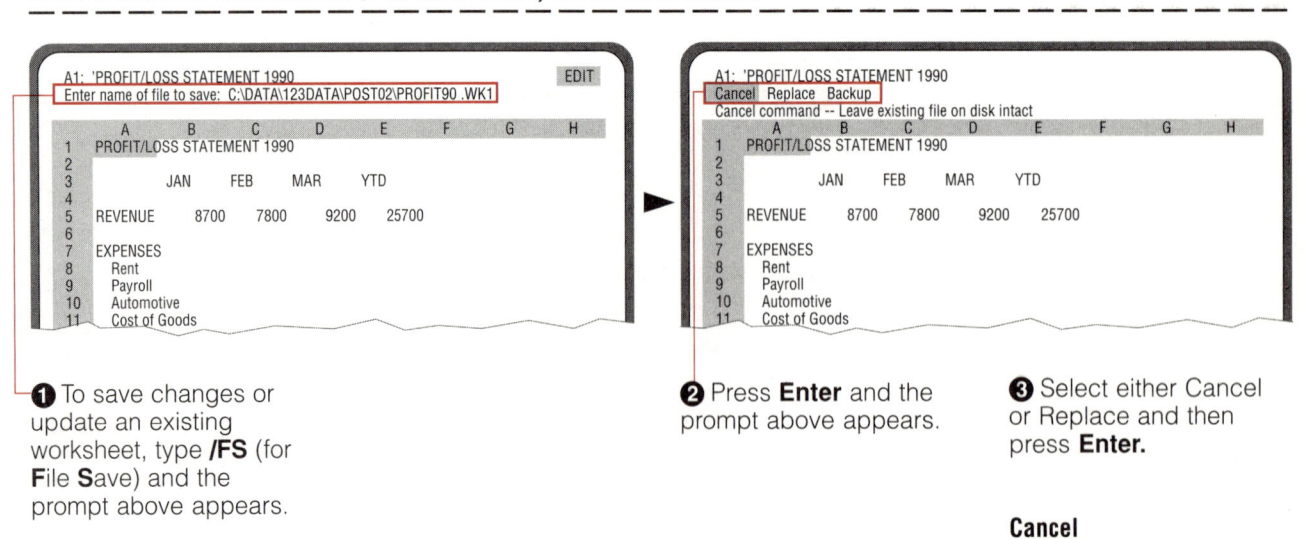

❶ To save changes or update an existing worksheet, type **/FS** (for **F**ile **S**ave) and the prompt above appears.

❷ Press **Enter** and the prompt above appears.

❸ Select either Cancel or Replace and then press **Enter.**

Cancel
Leaves existing file on disk intact.

Replace
Updates the file on disk with the current file.

18

DIRECTORIES | CHANGE THE DEFAULT DIRECTORY | DISPLAY THE FILENAME | **SAVE A WORKSHEET** | RETRIEVE A WORKSHEET | ERASE A WORKSHEET

CREATE AND EDIT A WORKSHEET

MANAGE YOUR FILES

WORK WITH RANGES

WORK WITH FORMULAS

FORMAT A WORKSHEET

CREATE AND SORT A DATABASE

PRINTING

GRAPHING

HELP

Clear the screen

Press **/WEY** (for **W**orksheet **E**rase **Y**es).

This command clears the screen so that a new worksheet can be created.

Note: Before using this command, save the worksheet if it has been changed or just recently created.

❹ Type the name of the file (example: PROFIT90) and press **Enter**.

● The worksheet PROFIT90 is saved to the POST02 subdirectory.

Note: 1-2-3 automatically adds an extension of .wk1 to the file (example: PROFIT90.WK1).

SAVE A REVISED WORKSHEET *(to a new directory with a different name)*

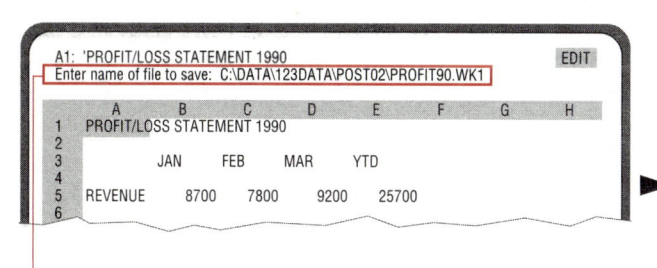

❶ To save a revised worksheet to a new directory with a different name, type **/FS** (for **F**ile **S**ave) and the prompt above appears.

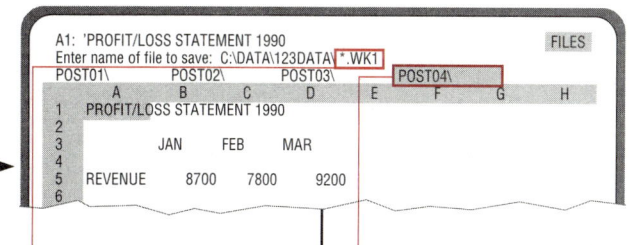

❷ Press **Esc** and POST02\PROFIT90.WK1 is replaced by *.wk1

❸ Highlight the subdirectory required (example: POST 04) and press **Enter**.

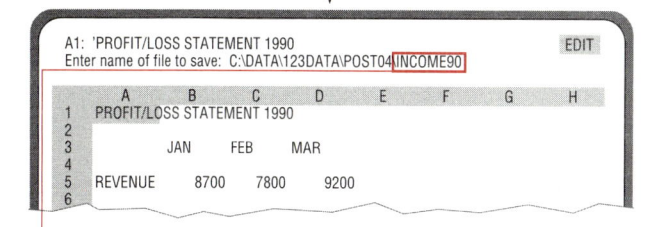

❹ Type the new filename (example: INCOME90) and press **Enter**.

● The revised file PROFIT90 is saved to the POST04 subdirectory.

19

RETRIEVE A WORKSHEET

ERASE A WORKSHEET

RETRIEVE A WORKSHEET *(that has been previously saved)*

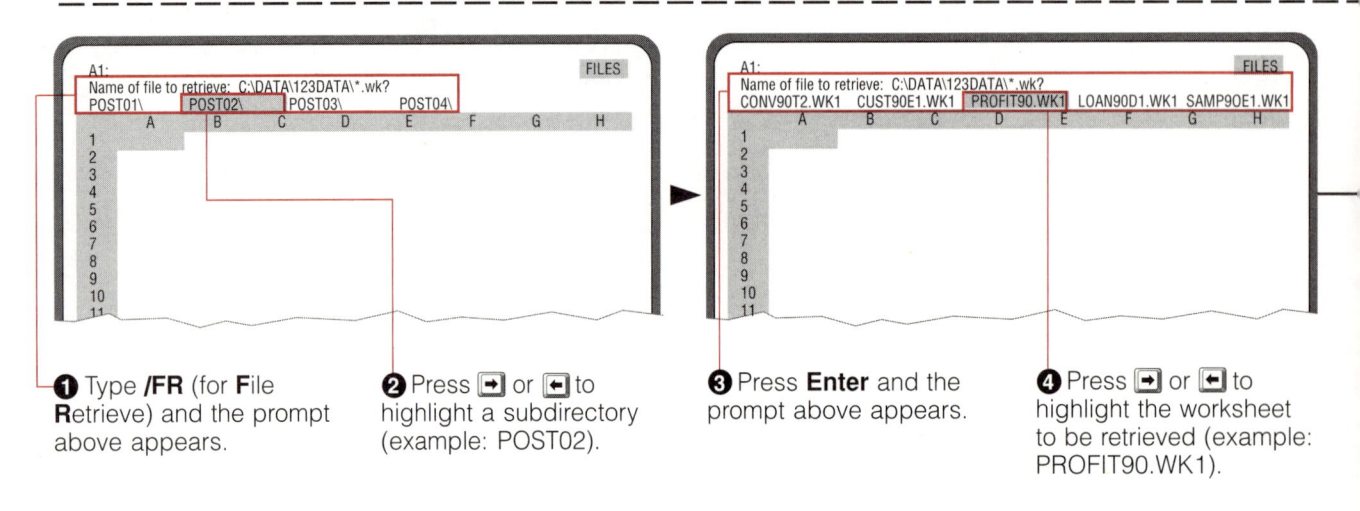

❶ Type **/FR** (for **F**ile **R**etrieve) and the prompt above appears.

❷ Press → or ← to highlight a subdirectory (example: POST02).

❸ Press **Enter** and the prompt above appears.

❹ Press → or ← to highlight the worksheet to be retrieved (example: PROFIT90.WK1).

ERASE A WORKSHEET *(CAUTION: This command **permanently** erases the file from your hard disk.)*

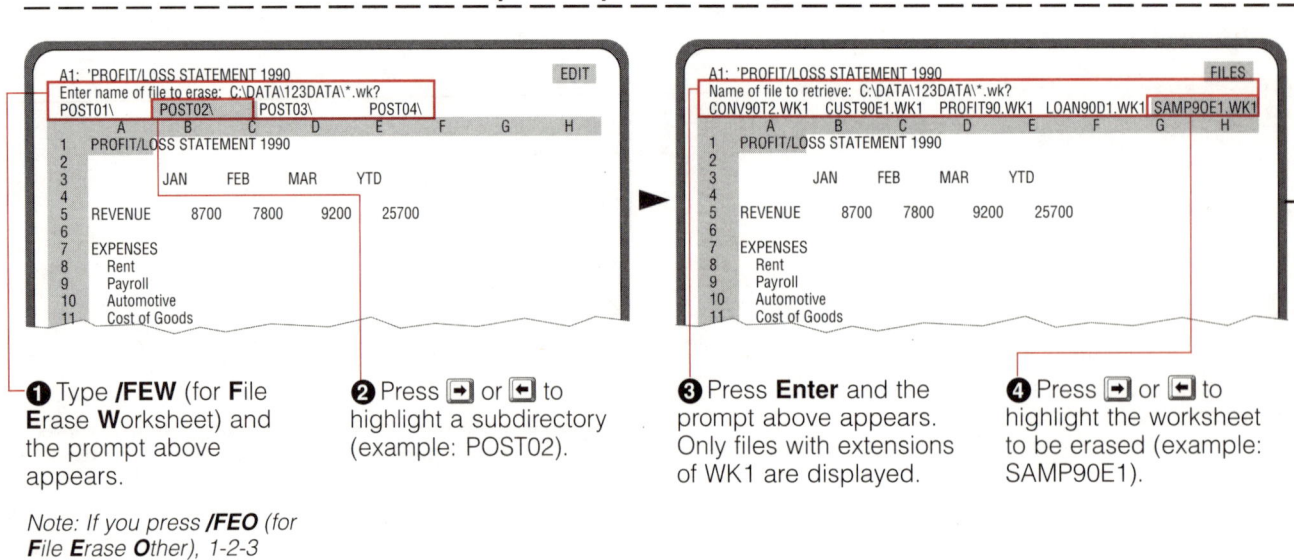

❶ Type **/FEW** (for **F**ile **E**rase **W**orksheet) and the prompt above appears.

*Note: If you press **/FEO** (for **F**ile **E**rase **O**ther), 1-2-3 displays all files in the subdirectory chosen.*

❷ Press → or ← to highlight a subdirectory (example: POST02).

❸ Press **Enter** and the prompt above appears. Only files with extensions of WK1 are displayed.

❹ Press → or ← to highlight the worksheet to be erased (example: SAMP90E1).

20

| DIRECTORIES | CHANGE THE DEFAULT DIRECTORY | DISPLAY THE FILENAME | SAVE A WORKSHEET | **RETRIEVE A WORKSHEET** | **ERASE A WORKSHEET** |

MANAGE YOUR FILES

CREATE AND EDIT A WORKSHEET

WORK WITH RANGES

WORK WITH FORMULAS

FORMAT A WORKSHEET

CREATE AND SORT A DATABASE

PRINTING

GRAPHING

HELP

❺ Press **Enter** and the PROFIT90.WK1 worksheet appears on screen.

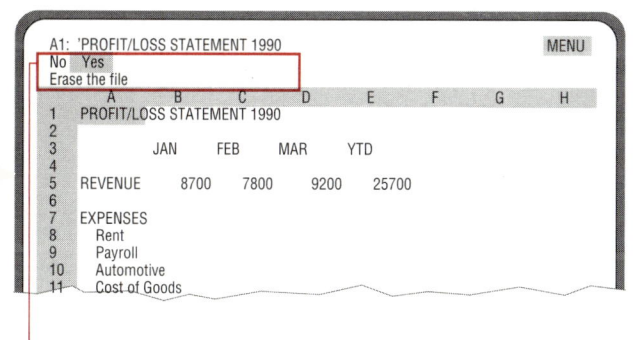

❺ Press **Enter** and the prompt above appears.

❻ Press **N** to cancel the command.

or

Press **Y** to erase the file.

Note: The data displayed on the screen remains intact. Type /WEY to clear the screen so that a new file can be created.

Worksheets on floppy disks

If a worksheet must be stored (or has been stored) on a floppy disk—its file location must be specified in order to work with it.

❶ When the prompt *"C:\DATA\123DATA*.WK1"* appears, press **ESC** enough times to clear the full path off the screen.

❷ To identify the floppy disk, type **A:** and press **Enter**.

❸ Follow the normal sequence of File Management steps such as select a subdirectory, or save\retrieve\erase a worksheet.

21

INTRODUCTION

A range is a rectangular block of cells that 1-2-3 treats as a unit.

Ranges allow 1-2-3 to copy, move, erase and print information efficiently.

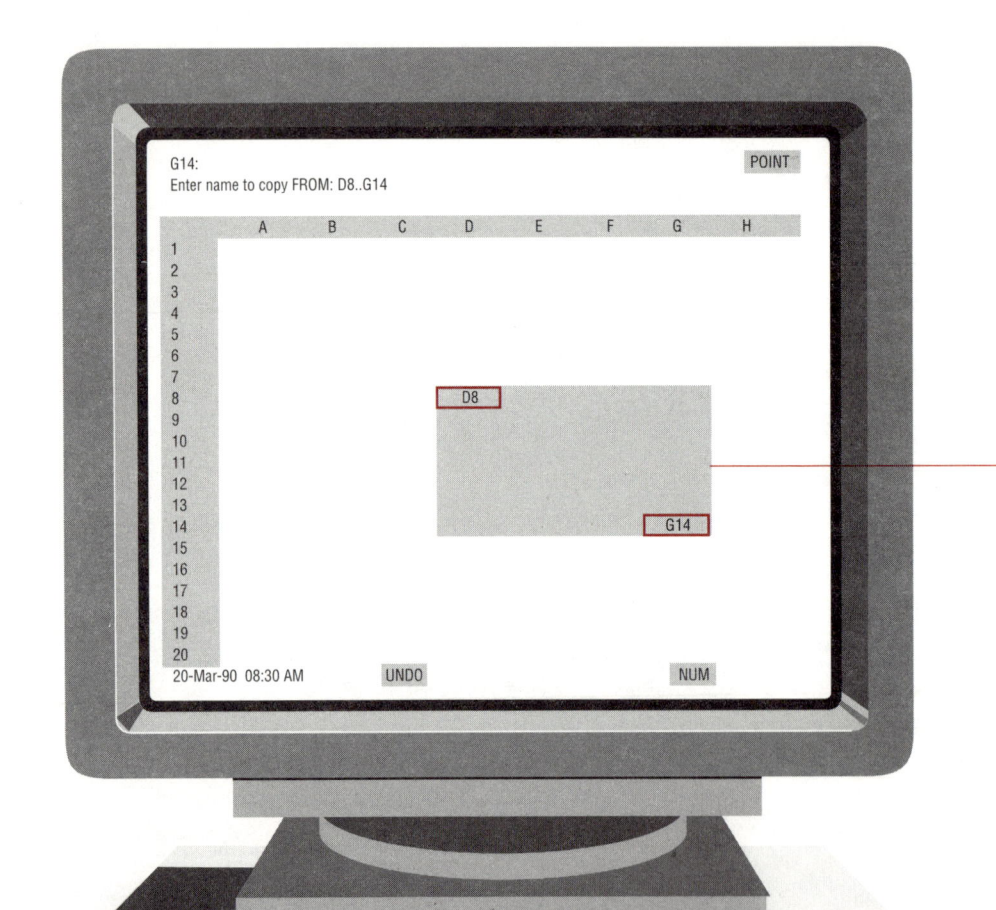

● A range is defined by the two most distant cell addresses (example: D8..G14).

Note: A range can only be square or rectangular in shape.

| INTRODUCTION | COPY A RANGE | MOVE OR ERASE A RANGE | THE UNDO FUNCTION | SEARCH A RANGE | FIND OR REPLACE A STRING |

RANGE EXAMPLES

Ranges can be specified two ways:

By typing

To specify a range, type the top left cell address followed by a . (period) and then the bottom right cell address (example: **J11.M18**).

Note: When you type a range, only one . (period) is required. When 1-2-3 identifies a range, it uses two periods (..).

With the arrow keys

Move the cell pointer to the top left cell address of the range (example: **J11**). Type . (period) to anchor the range. Press the arrow keys until the entire range is selected or painted (example: **J11..M18**).

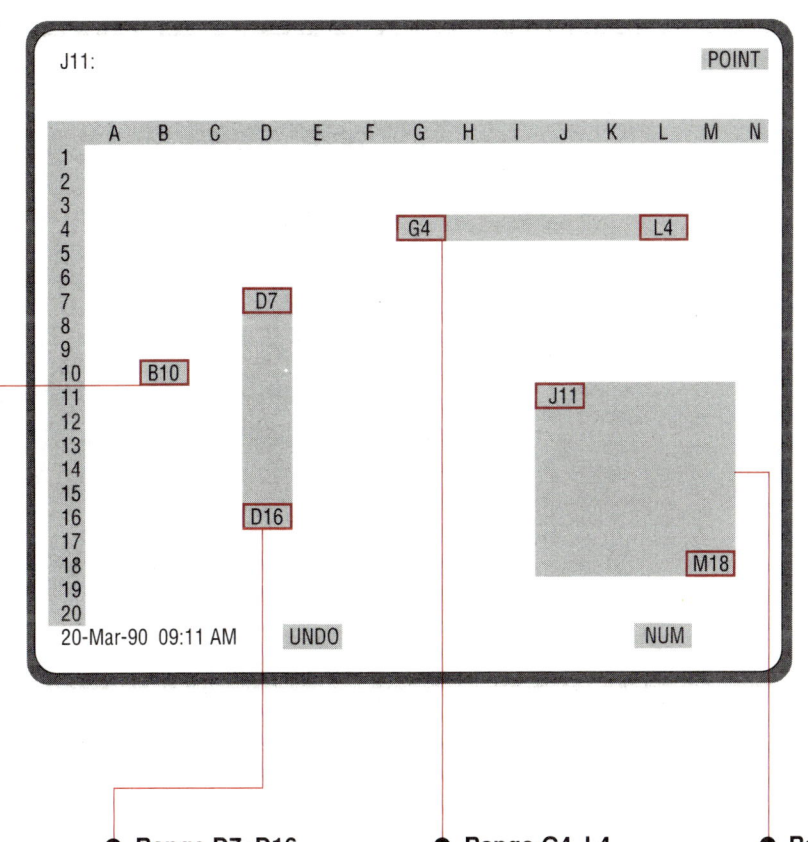

Note: To specify a range you first must select a command such as Copy, Move Erase, etc.

- **Range B10..B10**
This range defines a single cell. The start and end cell addresses of the range **B10..B10** are identical.

- **Range D7..D16**
This range defines a column. The start cell address is **D7** and the end cell address is **D16**.

- **Range G4..L4**
This range defines a row. The start cell address is **G4** and the end cell address is **L4**.

- **Range J11..M18**
This range defines a rectangular block. The start cell address is **J11** and the end cell address is **M18**.

CREATE AND EDIT A WORKSHEET

MANAGE YOUR FILES

WORK WITH RANGES

WORK WITH FORMULAS

FORMAT A WORKSHEET

CREATE AND SORT A DATABASE

PRINTING

GRAPHING

HELP

23

COPY A RANGE

RULES FOR COPYING

- The Copy command is used to copy data (labels or values) into a different part of the worksheet.
- Before beginning the Copy command, you must know where the data is coming **FROM** and where it is going **TO**.
- A range can only contain a square or rectangular group of cells.
- A range can consist of only one cell.

COPYING DATA FROM ONE CELL INTO ONE OTHER CELL

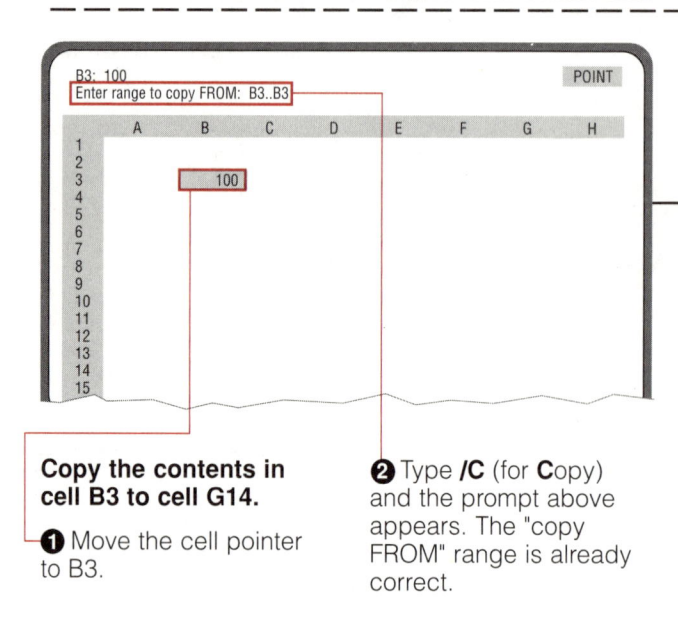

Copy the contents in cell B3 to cell G14.

❶ Move the cell pointer to B3.

❷ Type **/C** (for **C**opy) and the prompt above appears. The "copy FROM" range is already correct.

COPYING DATA FROM ONE CELL INTO MANY CELLS

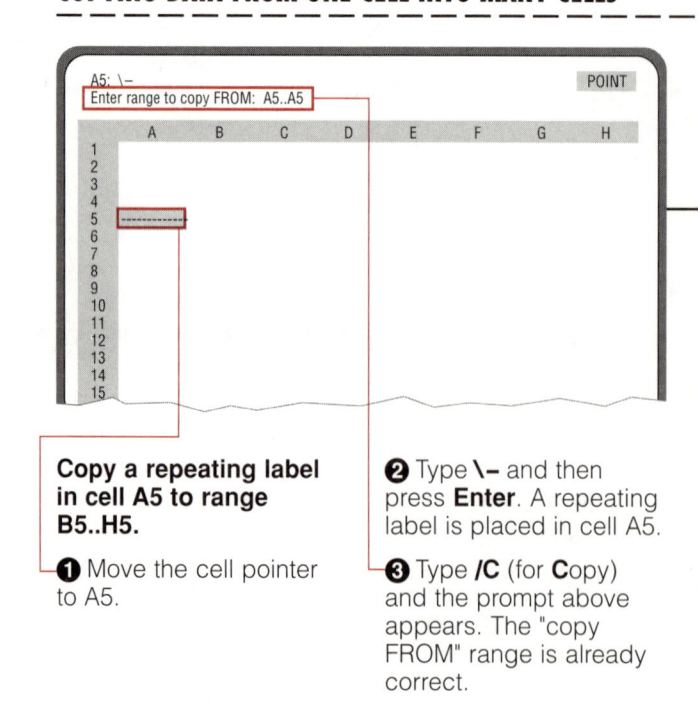

Copy a repeating label in cell A5 to range B5..H5.

❶ Move the cell pointer to A5.

❷ Type **\−** and then press **Enter**. A repeating label is placed in cell A5.

❸ Type **/C** (for **C**opy) and the prompt above appears. The "copy FROM" range is already correct.

24

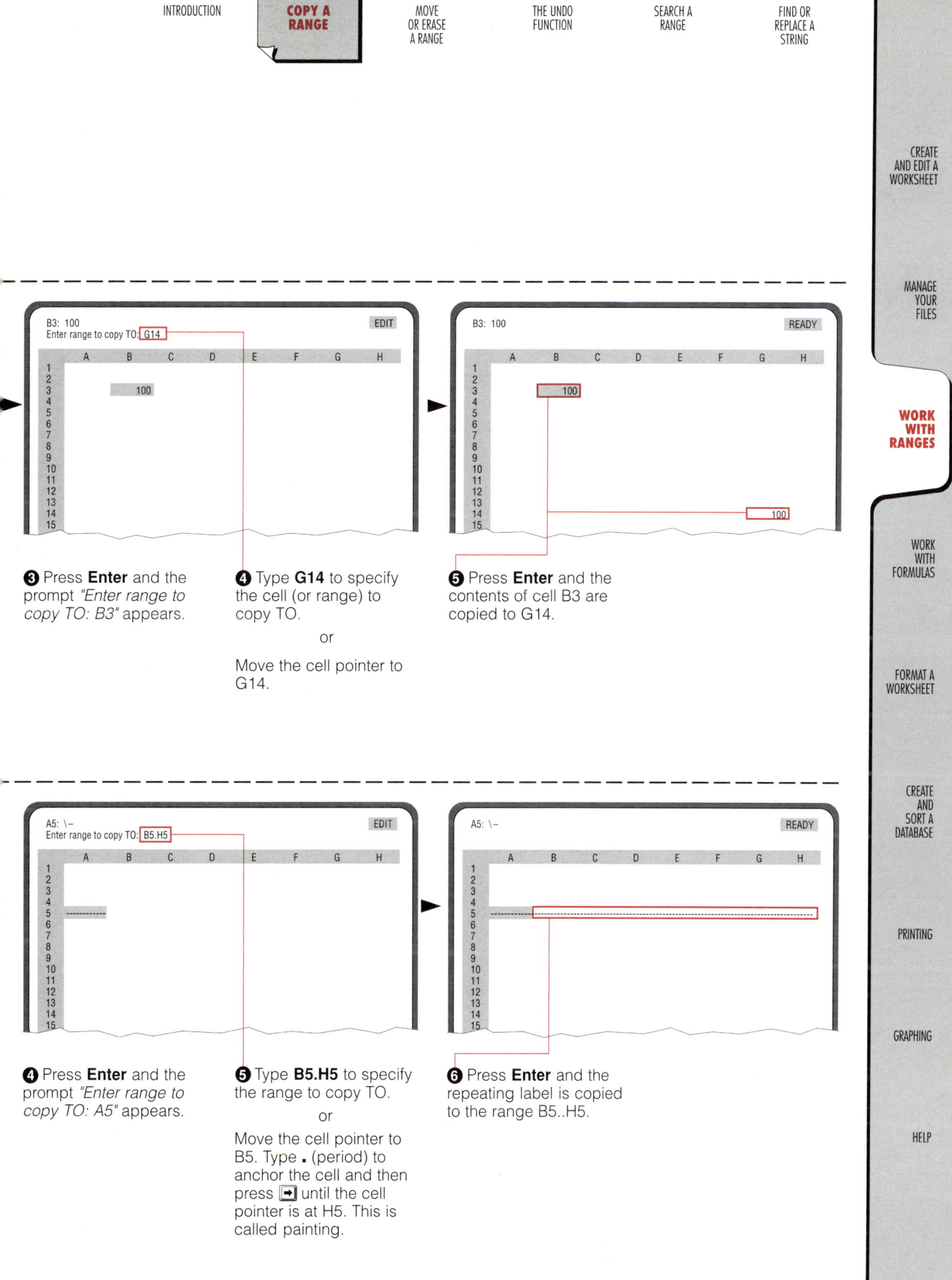

INTRODUCTION | **COPY A RANGE** | MOVE OR ERASE A RANGE | THE UNDO FUNCTION | SEARCH A RANGE | FIND OR REPLACE A STRING

CREATE AND EDIT A WORKSHEET

MANAGE YOUR FILES

WORK WITH RANGES

WORK WITH FORMULAS

FORMAT A WORKSHEET

CREATE AND SORT A DATABASE

PRINTING

GRAPHING

HELP

❸ Press **Enter** and the prompt *"Enter range to copy TO: B3"* appears.

❹ Type **G14** to specify the cell (or range) to copy TO.

or

Move the cell pointer to G14.

❺ Press **Enter** and the contents of cell B3 are copied to G14.

❹ Press **Enter** and the prompt *"Enter range to copy TO: A5"* appears.

❺ Type **B5.H5** to specify the range to copy TO.

or

Move the cell pointer to B5. Type **.** (period) to anchor the cell and then press ➡ until the cell pointer is at H5. This is called painting.

❻ Press **Enter** and the repeating label is copied to the range B5..H5.

25

COPY A RANGE

COPYING DATA FROM A RANGE OF CELLS INTO ANOTHER RANGE OF CELLS

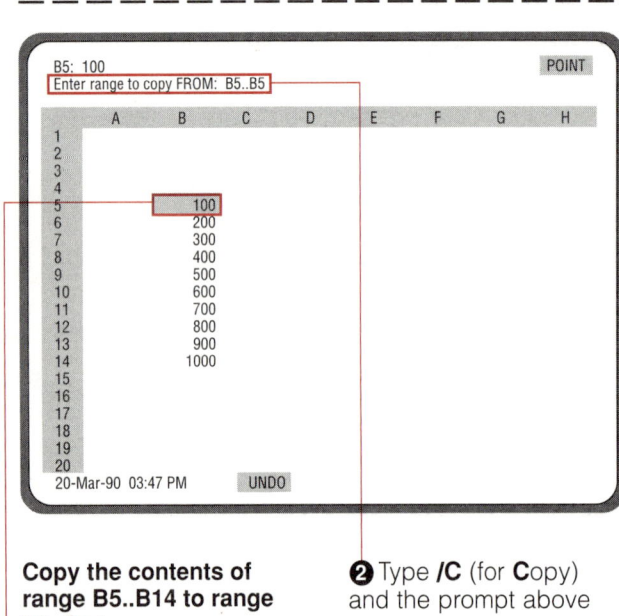

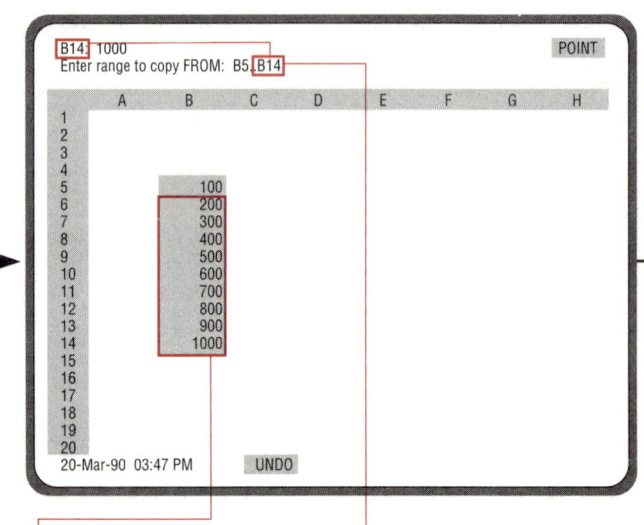

Copy the contents of range B5..B14 to range F5..G14.

❶ Move the cell pointer to B5.

❷ Type **/C** (for **C**opy) and the prompt above appears.

❸ Press ⬇ until the cell pointer is at the end of range.

or

Type the first cell address in the range, followed by **.** (period), and then the last cell of the range (example: B5.B14).

● Each time ⬇ is pressed, the cell address changes.

Anchoring and painting a range

Type **.** (period) to anchor a range. Then paint the range by moving the cell pointer to the end of the range.

Typing **.** (period) is called anchoring. It allows a range to be painted (or highlighted) using the arrow keys.

To unanchor a range, press **Esc**.

INTRODUCTION | **COPY A RANGE** | MOVE OR ERASE A RANGE | THE UNDO FUNCTION | SEARCH A RANGE | FIND OR REPLACE A STRING

---

4 Press **Enter** and the prompt *"Enter range to copy TO: B5"* appears.

5 Move the cell pointer to F5. This is the first cell into which the range will be copied.

6 Type the range F5.G5.

or

Type **.** (period) to anchor the cell pointer in that cell. The prompt changes to *"Enter range to copy TO: F5..F5"*. Press ➡ to paint (or highlight) the range F5..G5.

Note: You only have to paint the top cells into which the range will be copied. It is not necessary to paint the entire range of cells.

7 Press **Enter** and the range B5..B14 is copied to range F5..G14.

Note: If formulas are part of the range, they are also copied by this command.

Changing the anchor cell

The anchor cell can be changed to any corner of a range. *Remember the range is painted relative to the anchor cell.*

Type **.** (period) to move the anchor cell clockwise one corner position. Repeat until the desired corner is reached.

For horizontal or vertical ranges one cell wide, type **.** (period) twice.

Note: The cursor always appears opposite the anchored cell corner.

CREATE AND EDIT A WORKSHEET

MANAGE YOUR FILES

WORK WITH RANGES

WORK WITH FORMULAS

FORMAT A WORKSHEET

CREATE AND SORT A DATABASE

PRINTING

GRAPHING

HELP

27

MOVE OR ERASE A RANGE

THE UNDO FUNCTION

MOVE A RANGE

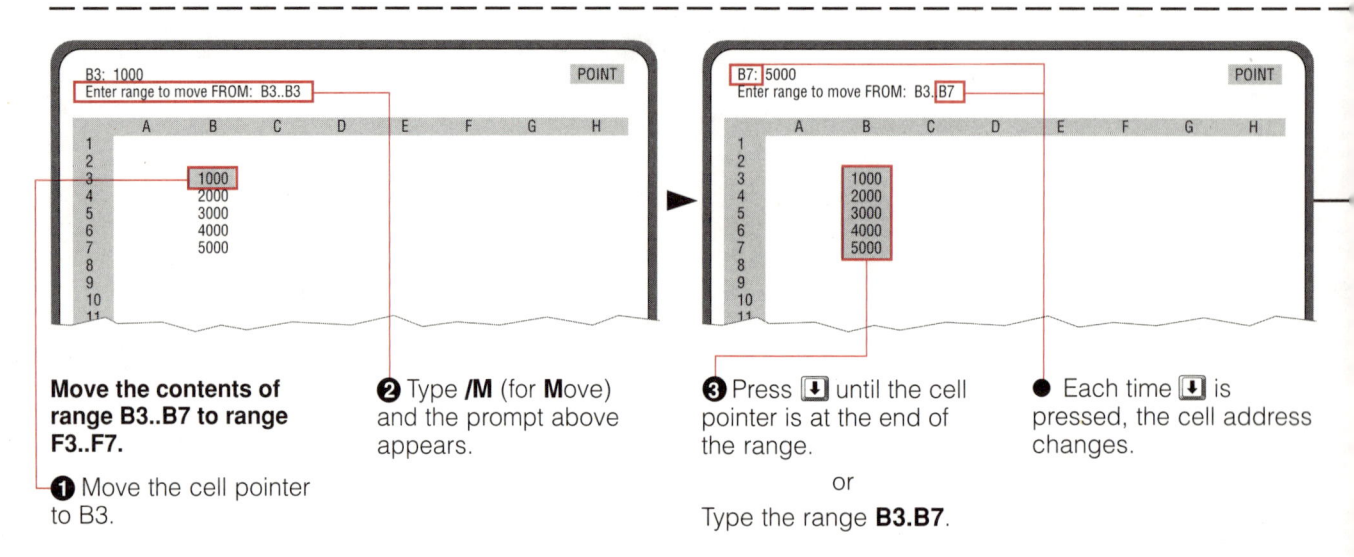

Move the contents of range B3..B7 to range F3..F7.

❶ Move the cell pointer to B3.

❷ Type **/M** (for **M**ove) and the prompt above appears.

❸ Press ↓ until the cell pointer is at the end of the range.

or

Type the range **B3.B7**.

● Each time ↓ is pressed, the cell address changes.

ERASE A RANGE

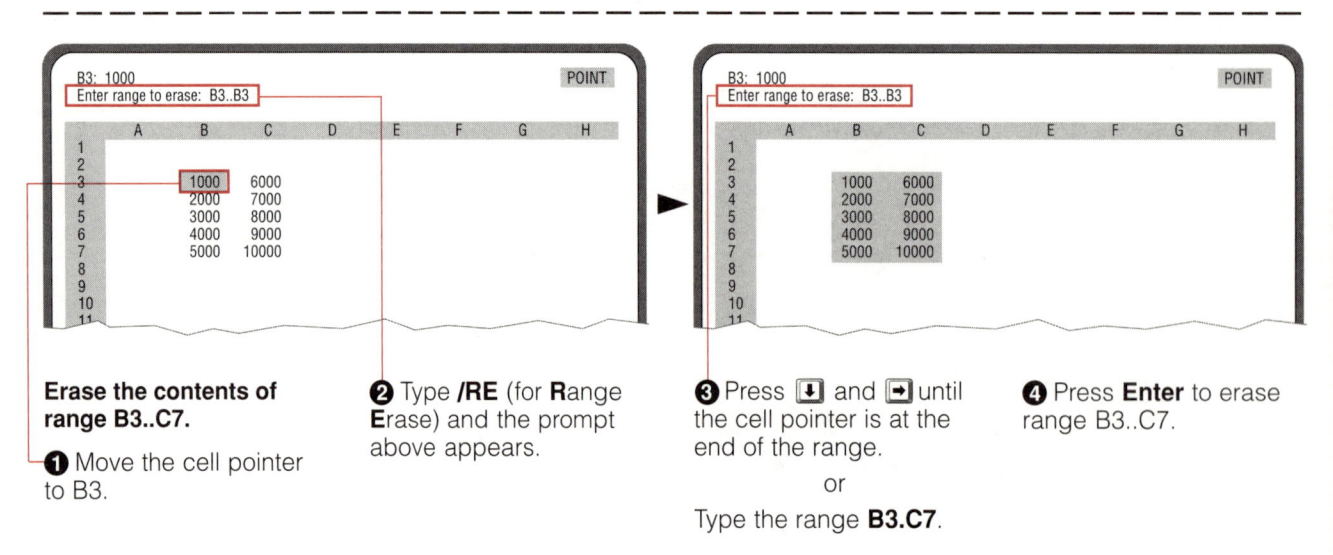

Erase the contents of range B3..C7.

❶ Move the cell pointer to B3.

❷ Type **/RE** (for **R**ange **E**rase) and the prompt above appears.

❸ Press ↓ and → until the cell pointer is at the end of the range.

or

Type the range **B3.C7**.

❹ Press **Enter** to erase range B3..C7.

28

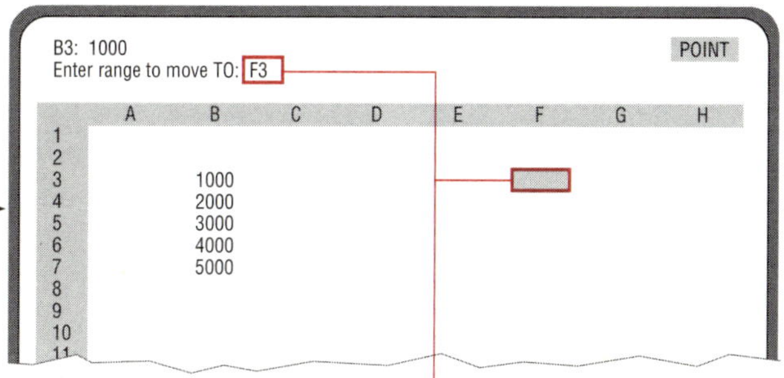

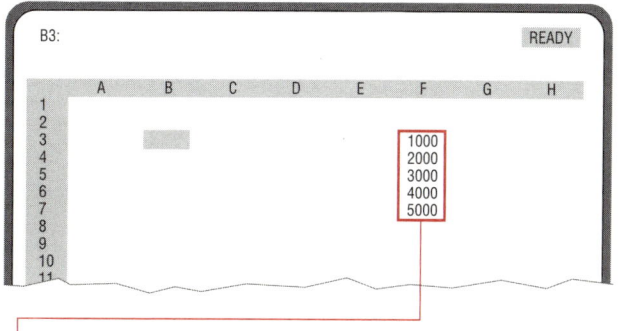

| INTRODUCTION | COPY A RANGE | **MOVE OR ERASE A RANGE** | **THE UNDO FUNCTION** | SEARCH A RANGE | FIND OR REPLACE A STRING |

❹ Press **Enter** and the prompt *"Enter range to move TO: B3"* appears.

❺ Move the cell pointer to F3. This is the top cell into which the range will be moved.

or

Type **F3**.

❻ Press **Enter** and the range B3..B7 is moved to range F3..F7.

Note: If formulas are part of the range, they are also moved by this command.

THE UNDO FUNCTION

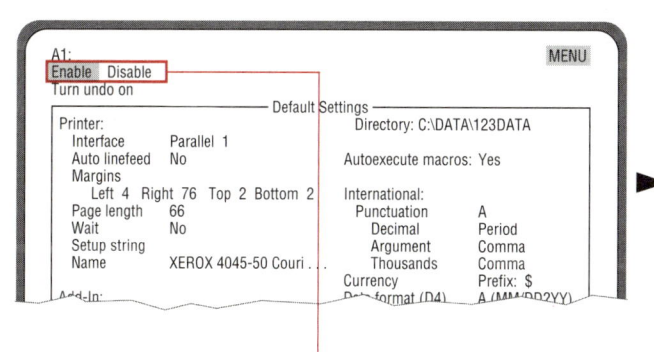

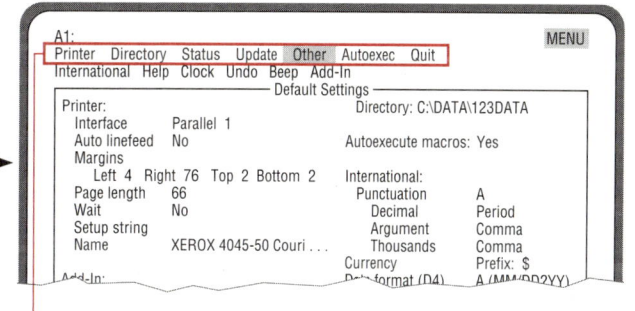

The UNDO function Alt-F4 cancels the most recent operation that altered the worksheet data.

For example, pressing **Alt-F4** restores the range that was just erased.

Note: To be used, the UNDO function must be "on". If it is not "on"—the word UNDO does not appear at the bottom of the screen.

❶ To turn "on" the UNDO function, press **/WGDOU** (for **W**orksheet **G**lobal **D**efault **O**ther **U**ndo) and the prompt above appears.

❷ Press **E** (for **E**nable) and the prompt above appears.

❸ Press **Q** (for **Q**uit) to return to the worksheet.

or

To make this the default setting for future sessions, type **UQ** (for **U**pdate **Q**uit).

Note: The UNDO function only works if 1-2-3 is in the READY mode.

*If **Alt-F4** is pressed once, pressing it a second time will UNDO the last UNDO operation.*

CREATE AND EDIT A WORKSHEET

MANAGE YOUR FILES

WORK WITH RANGES

WORK WITH FORMULAS

FORMAT A WORKSHEET

CREATE AND SORT A DATABASE

PRINTING

GRAPHING

HELP

29

SEARCH A RANGE | **FIND OR REPLACE A STRING**

SEARCH A RANGE

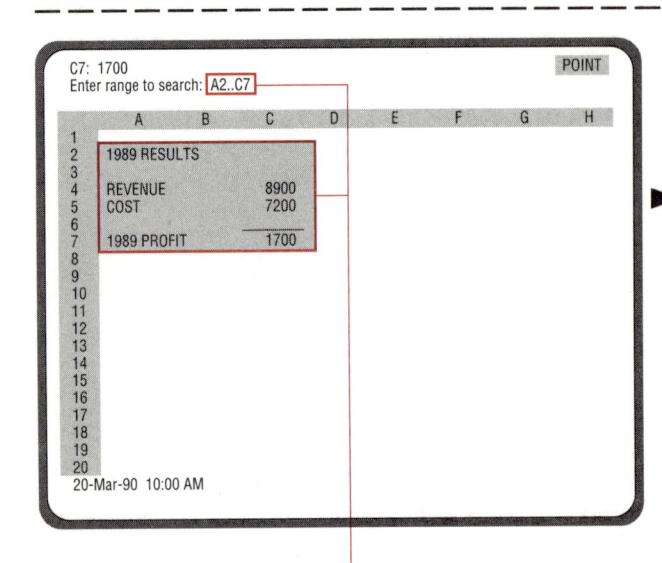

The search command allows you to identify strings (containing letters or numbers) in labels and/or formulas. The search is limited to the range you specify.

The search will only find numbers in a formula. It will not find numbers in values.

Note: The search is not case sensitive. Searching for b will find either b or B.

Set up the search range to find or replace the "89" string.

❶ Type **/RS** (for **R**ange **S**earch) and the prompt *"Enter range to search"* appears.

❷ Move the cell pointer to A2 (the beginning of the range). Type **.** (period) to anchor the range and then move the cell pointer to C7 (the end of the range).

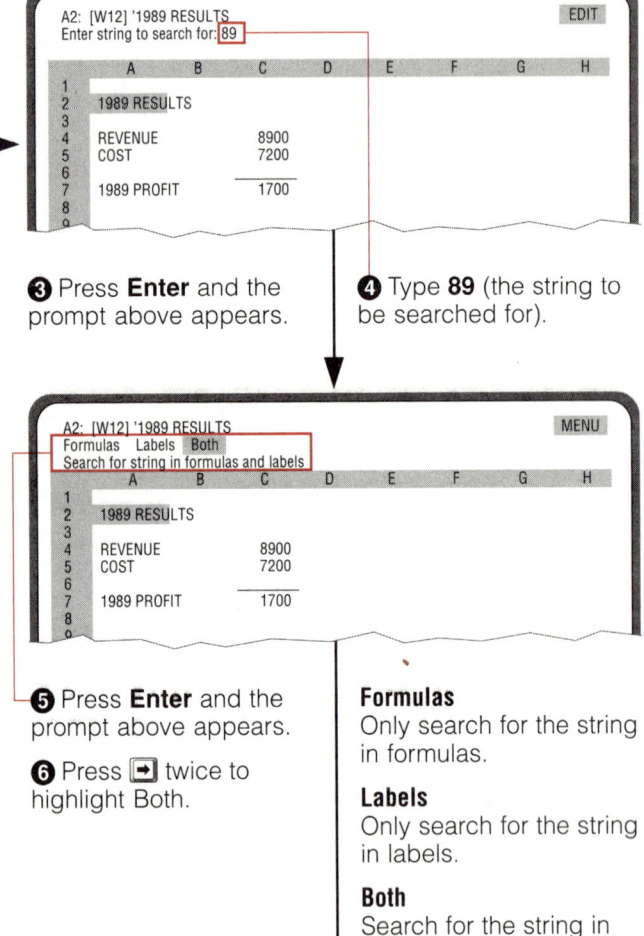

❸ Press **Enter** and the prompt above appears.

❹ Type **89** (the string to be searched for).

❺ Press **Enter** and the prompt above appears.

❻ Press ➡ twice to highlight Both.

Formulas
Only search for the string in formulas.

Labels
Only search for the string in labels.

Both
Search for the string in both formulas and labels.

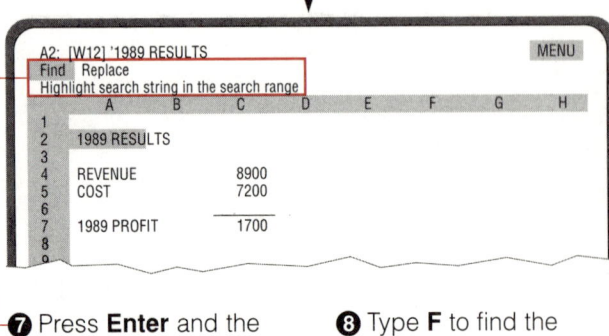

❼ Press **Enter** and the prompt above appears.

❽ Type **F** to find the string.

or

Type **R** to replace the string.

30

FIND THE STRING

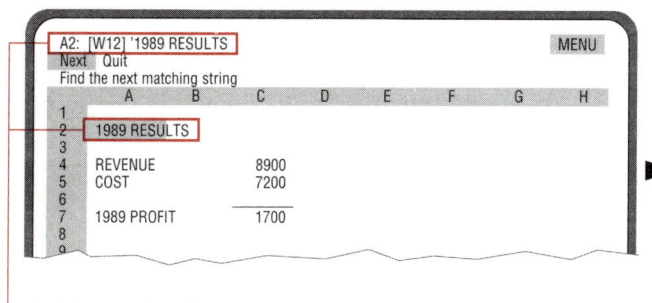

❶ After typing **F** (for **F**ind) the cell pointer moves to cell A2, the first occurrence of **89**.

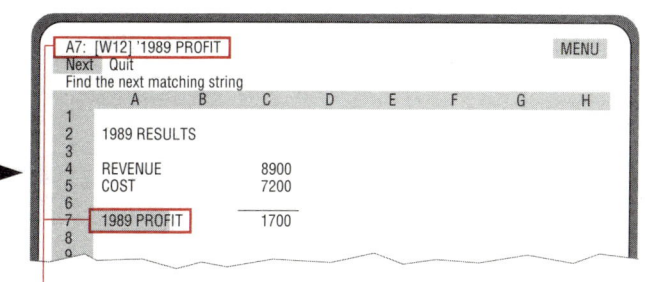

❷ Type **N** (for **N**ext) to find the next occurrence of **89**.

or

Type **Q** (for **Q**uit) to stop the search process.

*Note: If you press **N** and no further occurrences of **89** are found, the message "No more matching strings" appears. Press **Esc** to get out of the ERROR mode.*

REPLACE THE STRING

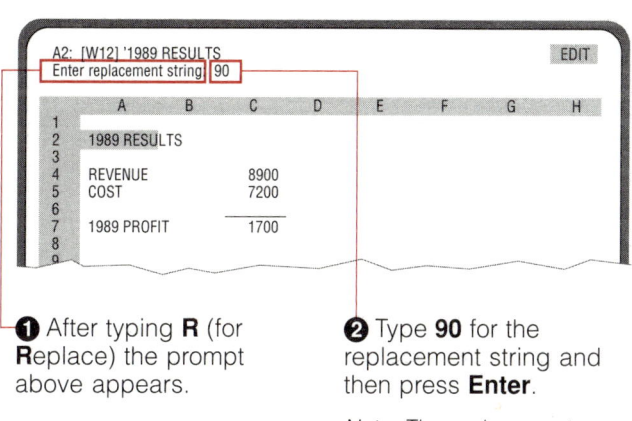

❶ After typing **R** (for **R**eplace) the prompt above appears.

❷ Type **90** for the replacement string and then press **Enter**.

Note: The replacement string is case sensitive (example: the replacement string AaBb replaces exactly as typed).

● At the first occurrence of **89**, the prompt above appears.

❸ Type **R** (for **R**eplace) to replace this string and go on to the next one.

or

Type **A** (for **A**ll) to replace all occurrences of the string.

or

Type **N** (for **N**ext) to leave this string as is and proceed to the next occurrence.

or

Type **Q** (for **Q**uit) to end the replace operation.

INTRODUCTION

- A formula performs calculations and contains mathematical operators, numbers and cell addresses.

- A formula begins with a number (0 through 9) or symbol + – (@ . $.

- The formula appears at the top of the screen when the cell pointer is at the cell containing the formula (example: B11).

- A formula can contain numbers and/or cell addresses.

- Cell addresses are used so that if the data in a cell changes, a formula somewhere else in the worksheet will not have to be altered.

- The result of the calculation appears at the cell containing the formula (example: B11).

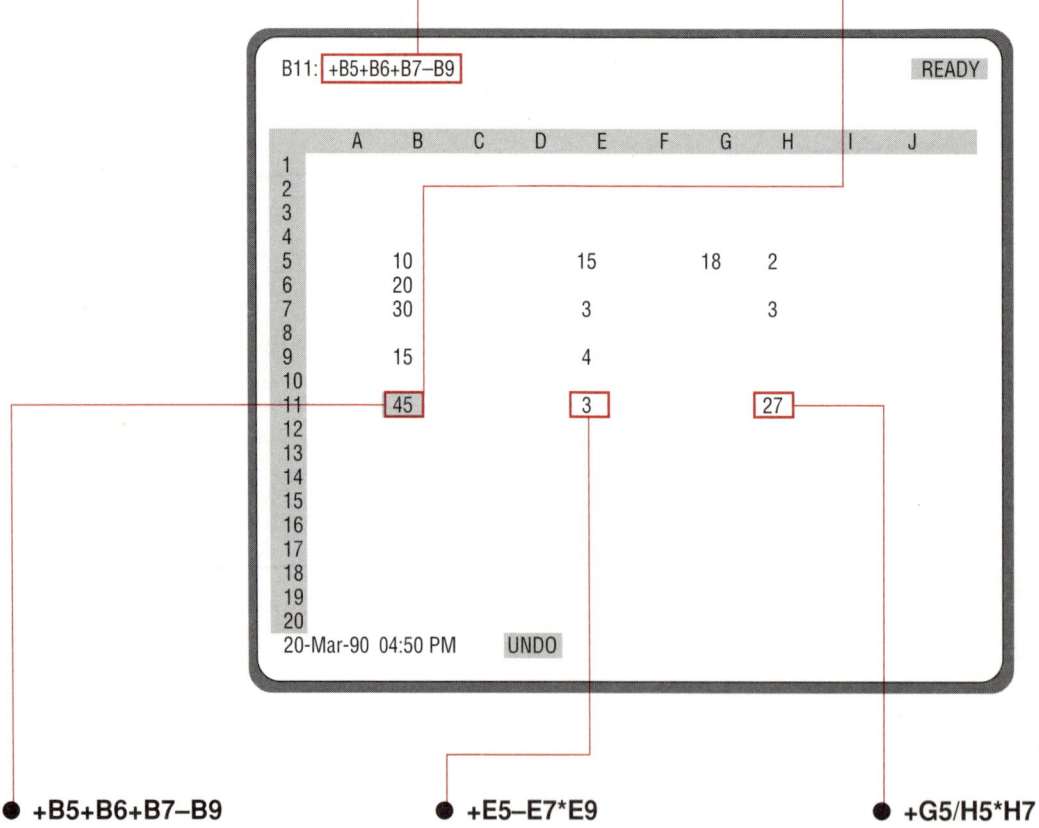

```
B11: +B5+B6+B7–B9                                READY

       A    B    C    D    E    F    G    H    I    J
 1
 2
 3
 4
 5         10             15        18    2
 6         20
 7         30              3         3
 8
 9         15              4
10
11         45              3              27
12
13
14
15
16
17
18
19
20
20-Mar-90  04:50 PM   UNDO
```

- **+B5+B6+B7–B9**

  The cell address B11 contains this formula.

  If: B5 = 10
        B6 = 20
        B7 = 30
        B9 = 15

  Then: The formula calculates 45.

  B11=10+20+30–15=45

- **+E5–E7*E9**

  The cell address E11 contains this formula.

  If: E5 = 15
        E7 = 3
        E9 = 4

  Then: The formula calculates 3.

  E11=15–3*4=3

- **+G5/H5*H7**

  The cell address H11 contains this formula.

  If: G5 = 18
        H5 = 2
        H7 = 3

  Then: The formula calculates 27.

  H11=18/2*3=27

ORDER OF PRECEDENCE

Operation	Order of Precedence
Multiplication	1 ⎤ Done in order
Division	1 ⎦ of appearance
Addition	2 ⎤ Done in order
Subtraction	2 ⎦ of appearance

Example:	15–3*4 is executed as follows: –3*4+15=3
Example:	18/2*3 is executed as follows: 18/2*3=27
Example:	1+2+3*4 is executed as follows: 3*4+1+2=15

- Mathematical operators are also included in formulas:

  - **+** Add
  - **–** Subtract
  - ***** Multiply
  - **/** Divide (a formula cannot begin with a division sign)

- 1-2-3 performs operations in formulas based on the order of precedence.

Overriding the order of precedence

To override the order of precedence, parenthesis can be used:

Examples:

Formula	Execution
E5–E7*E9	15–3*4=3
(E5–E7)*E9	(15–3)*4=48
+G5/H2*H7	18/2*3=27
G5/(H2*H7)	18/(2*3)=3
J5+J6+J7*J9	1+2+3*4=15
(J5+J6+J7)*J9	(1+2+3)*4=24

33

@FUNCTIONS

@Functions are formulas built into 1-2-3 to perform time-saving set-up procedures.

Although there are many kinds of @Functions, they all follow the same basic rules.

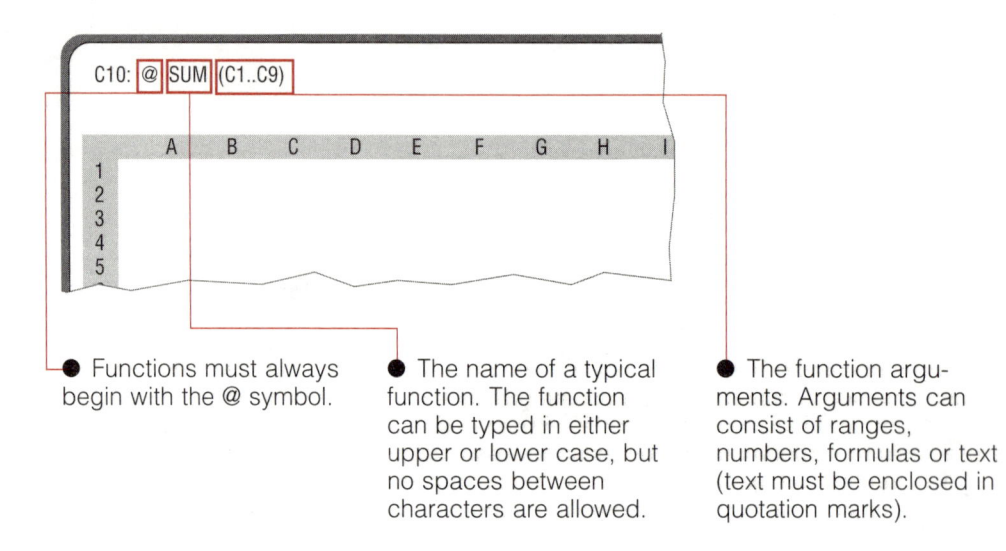

C10: @ SUM (C1..C9)

- Functions must always begin with the @ symbol.
- The name of a typical function. The function can be typed in either upper or lower case, but no spaces between characters are allowed.
- The function arguments. Arguments can consist of ranges, numbers, formulas or text (text must be enclosed in quotation marks).

TYPICAL @FUNCTIONS

@SUM	Adds together the data in a range of cells. *Example: @SUM(C1..C9)*	**@ROUND**	Rounds any value up to 15 decimal places. *Example: @ROUND(C2,1) where "1" is the number of decimal places.*
@DATE	Calculates the serial date number for any date after Dec 31,1899. *Example: @DATE(90,03,01) for March 1, 1990) = 32933*	**@MAX**	Finds the largest value in numbers or ranges. *Example: @MAX(B2..B70)*
@AVG	Averages the values of numbers or ranges. *Example: @AVG(B1..B6)*	**@MIN**	Finds the minimum value in numbers or ranges. *Example: @MIN(B2..B70)*

Note: For a complete list of @Functions refer to Lotus Reference Manual.

INTRODUCTION | **@FUNCTIONS** | RELATIVE CELL REFERENCES | ABSOLUTE CELL REFERENCES

@SUM FUNCTION

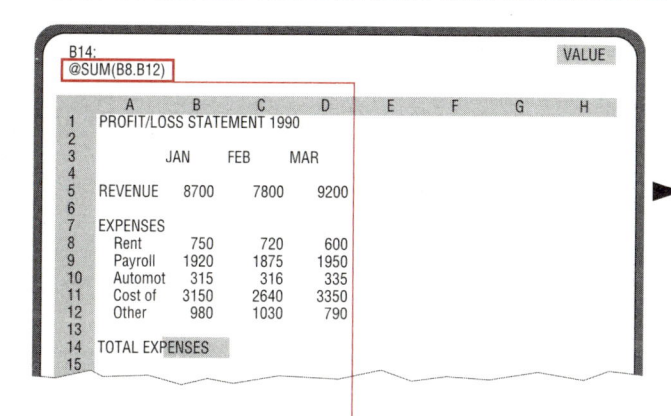

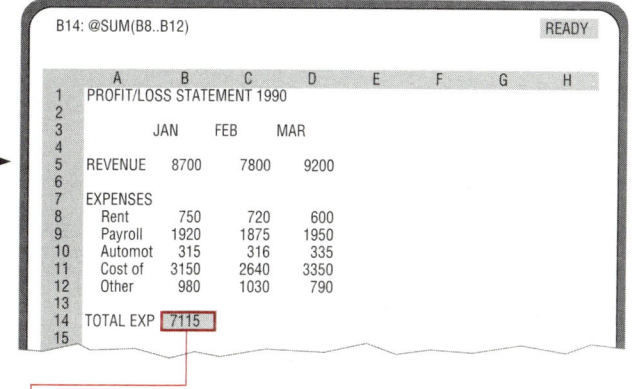

Add the range of cells B8 to B12 and place the sum in cell B14.

❶ Move the cell pointer to B14.

❷ Type **@SUM(B8.B12)**.

❸ Press **Enter** and the sum appears in cell B14.

Note: The @SUM function can also be used to add together random cells.

Example:

To add cells A1, A50, F7, G22, type **@SUM(A1,A50,F7,G22)**.

@DATE FUNCTION

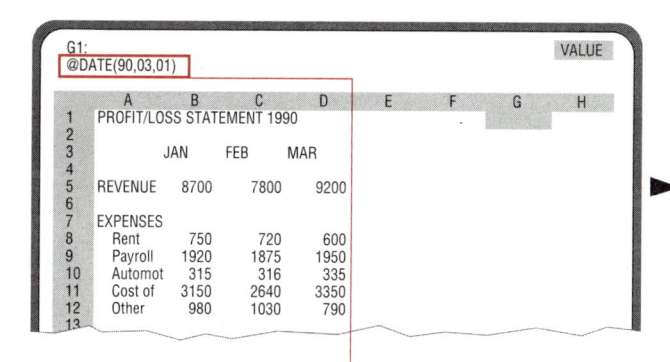

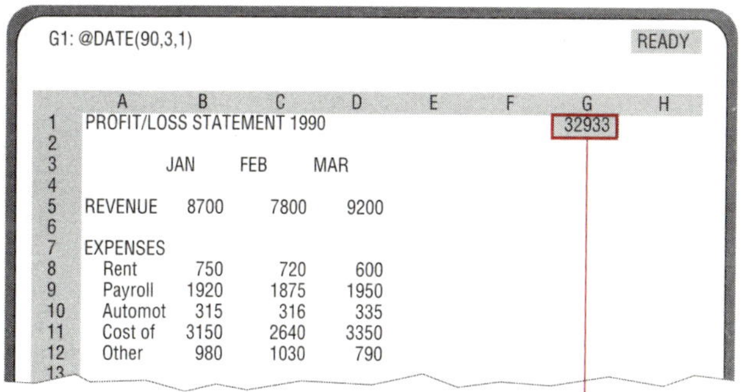

The @DATE function is used to key dates into a worksheet that will later be used for sorting, and calculating elapsed time.

The keying sequence is @DATE(YY,MM,DD).

❶ Move the cell pointer to G1.

❷ To key in March 1, 1990, type **@DATE(90,03,01)**.

❸ Press **Enter** and a serial date number of 32933 (the number of days since Dec 31, 1899) is placed in cell G1.

*Note: To format the serial number into a recognizable date, use the /**R**ange **F**ormat **D**ate command and the /**W**orksheet **C**olumn **S**et-width command.*

Even after formatting, the data can be used for sorting, calculating elapsed time, etc.

WORK WITH FORMULAS

RELATIVE CELL REFERENCES

ABSOLUTE CELL REFERENCES

RELATIVE CELL REFERENCES

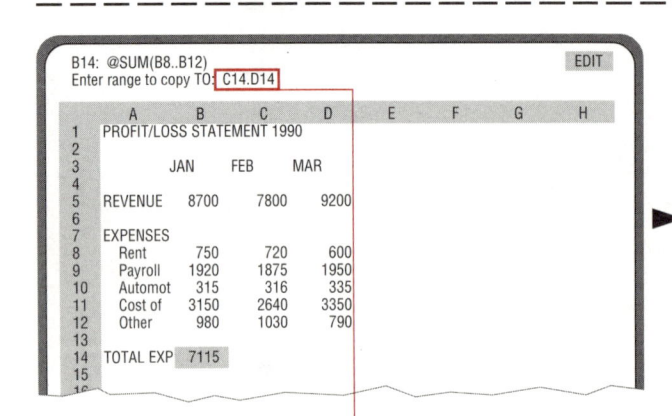

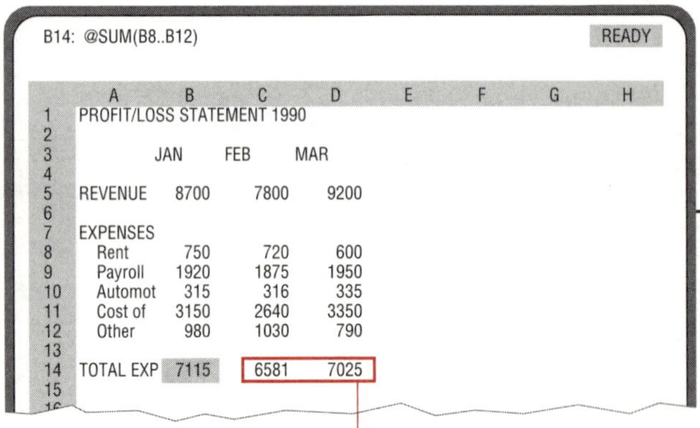

1-2-3 remembers cell addresses in a relative way. If a formula is copied to a range of cells, 1-2-3 adjusts the cell references automatically.

❶ Move the cell pointer to B14.

❷ Type **/C** (for **C**opy) and then press **Enter**.

❸ Type **C14.D14**.

❹ Press **Enter** and the function in cell B14 is copied to cells C14 and D14.

● The sums of 6581 in cell C14 and 7025 in cell D14 are correct because 1-2-3 adjusted the relative cell references during the copy process.

ABSOLUTE CELL REFERENCES

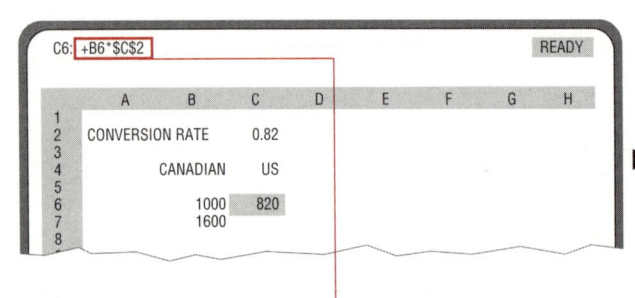

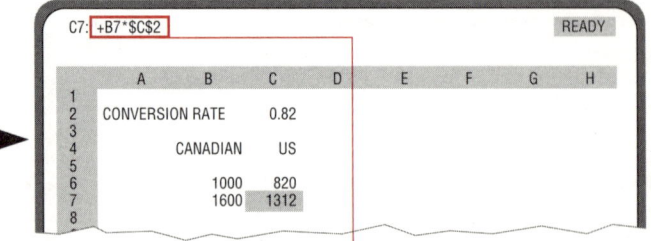

In this conversion rate example, the formula in cell B6 must be copied to B7.

Copying the formula from cell C6 (+B6*C2) to cell C7 (+B7*C3) using the relative cell reference, results in an error. This is because cell C3 is empty.

❶ Move the cell pointer to C6.

❷ Type the formula **+B6*C2** and then press **Enter**.

Note: The $ signs tell 1-2-3 that cell C2 is an absolute cell reference. This means the value of cell C2 (0.82) is fixed during the copying process.

❸ Type **/C** (for **C**opy) and then press **Enter**.

❹ Press ⬇ once and then press **Enter** to copy the formula in cell C6 to cell C7.

● Press ⬇ once to move to cell C7. The formula in cell C7 is now +B7*C2 or 1600x0.82=1312.

36

INTRODUCTION @FUNCTIONS **RELATIVE CELL REFERENCES** **ABSOLUTE CELL REFERENCES**

```
C14: @SUM(C8..C12)                                      READY
     A          B      C      D     E     F     G     H
 1  PROFIT/LOSS STATEMENT 1990
 2
 3              JAN    FEB    MAR
 4
 5  REVENUE    8700   7800   9200
 6
 7  EXPENSES
 8    Rent      750    720    600
 9    Payroll  1920   1875   1950
10    Automot   315    316    335
11    Cost of  3150   2640   3350
12    Other     980   1030    790
13
14  TOTAL EXP 7115   6581   7025
15
```

```
D14: @SUM(D8..D12)                                      READY
     A          B      C      D     E     F     G     H
 1  PROFIT/LOSS STATEMENT 1990
 2
 3              JAN    FEB    MAR
 4
 5  REVENUE    8700   7800   9200
 6
 7  EXPENSES
 8    Rent      750    720    600
 9    Payroll  1920   1875   1950
10    Automot   315    316    335
11    Cost of  3150   2640   3350
12    Other     980   1030    790
13
14  TOTAL EXP 7115   6581   7025
15
```

5 To prove this, press ➡ once to move to cell C14.

● 1-2-3 has adjusted the relative cell references of the @SUM (C8..C12) function for the C column.

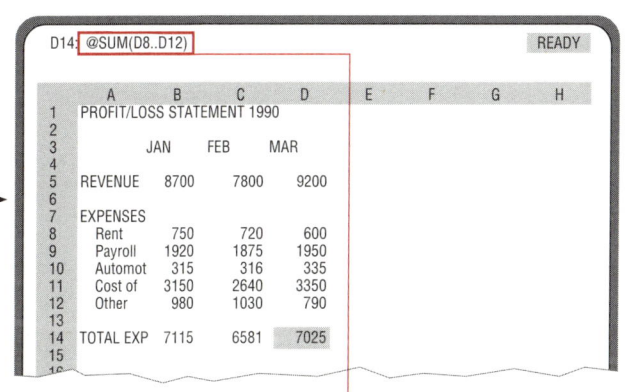

6 Press ➡ again to move to cell D14.

● 1-2-3 has adjusted the relative cell references of the @SUM (D8..D12) function for the D column.

Copying cells with absolute cell references

Example: +B6*C2.

The first $ sign tells 1-2-3 that the column in the cell reference address is fixed. The second $ sign tells 1-2-3 that the row in the cell reference address is also fixed during the copy process.

Shortcut to typing the $ signs

When typing or editing a formula, a cell reference can be converted from relative to absolute by pressing F4. The cursor must be on or to the right of the cell address as F4 is pressed.

To convert the cell reference back to absolute, press F4 three times.

Example: Change the cell reference of A1 from relative to absolute.

1 Type +A1 and then press F4. The cell reference is converted to +A1.

CREATE AND EDIT A WORKSHEET

MANAGE YOUR FILES

WORK WITH RANGES

WORK WITH FORMULAS

FORMAT A WORKSHEET

CREATE AND SORT A DATABASE

PRINTING

GRAPHING

HELP

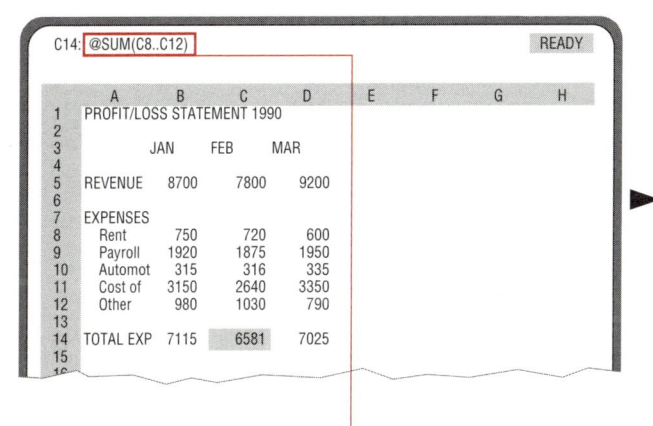

37

CHANGE CELL FORMAT

EXAMPLE: FORMAT ALL WORKSHEET VALUES AS , (COMMA)

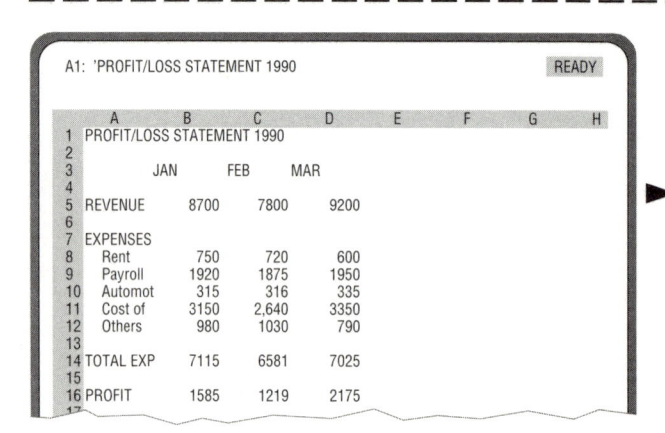

```
A1: 'PROFIT/LOSS STATEMENT 1990                                READY

      A         B      C      D     E    F    G    H
 1  PROFIT/LOSS STATEMENT 1990
 2
 3              JAN    FEB   MAR
 4
 5  REVENUE    8700   7800   9200
 6
 7  EXPENSES
 8    Rent      750    720    600
 9    Payroll  1920   1875   1950
10    Automot   315    316    335
11    Cost of  3150   2,640  3350
12    Others    980   1030    790
13
14  TOTAL EXP 7115   6581   7025
15
16  PROFIT   1585   1219   2175
17
```

```
A1: 'PROFIT/LOSS STATEMENT 1990                                READY
Fixed Sci Currency , General +/- Percent Date Text Hidden
Fixed number of decimal places (x.xx)
                      ─── Global Settings ───
Conventional memory:   183280 of 183280 Bytes (100%)
Expanded memory:       671416 of 884304 Bytes (75%)

Math coprocessor:      (None)

Recalculation:
  Method               Automatic
  Order                Natural
  Iterations           1

Circular reference:    (None)

Cell display:
  Format               (G)
  Label prefix         ' (left align)
  Column width         9
```

Format all values in the worksheet as , (Comma) with thousands separators and 2 decimal places.

Note: For other formats, use the same series of commands in this example, except select the required cell format in step 2.

❶ Press **/WGF** (for **W**orksheet **G**lobal **F**ormat) and the screen above appears listing the current Global Default Settings.

● A choice of cell formats is available (refer to chart below).

OTHER CELL FORMATS

Format	Description	No. of Decimals	Keyed	Shown As
, (Comma)	Values are displayed with thousands separators, up to 15 decimal places, parentheses or minus sign for negative values, leading zero for decimal values.	2 1 0 0	1000.56 7.5 2.0 −5.0	1,000.56 7.5 2 (5)
Currency	Values are displayed with a currency symbol, thousands separators, up to 15 decimal places, parentheses or minus sign for negative values, leading zero for decimal values.	2 0 0	1000.56 2.0 −5.5	$1,000.56 $2 ($6)
Fixed	Values are displayed with up to 15 decimal places, a minus sign for negative values, and a leading zero for decimal values.	2 1 0 0	1000 1000.00 1000.00 −1000	1000.00 1000.0 1000 −1000
General	Values are displayed with a minus sign for negatives, no thousands separators, no trailing zeros to the right of the decimal.		1000.00 −1000	1000 −1000
Percent	Values are displayed as percentages, with up to 15 decimal places and a percent.	2 1 0	.50 1.00 1.0	50.00% 100.0% 100%
Date	@DATE serial numbers are displayed as actual dates, in a variety of different formats depending on the selection made.	@DATE (90,05,04) Selection 1 @DATE (90,05,04) Selection 2 @DATE (90,05,04) Selection 3		04-May-90 04-May May-90

CHANGE CELL FORMAT

CHANGE COLUMN WIDTH ALIGN LABELS INSERT/DELETE ROWS OR COLUMNS

❷ Press **,** (for **C**omma Cell Format) and the prompt above appears.

Note: Any one of the other cell formats could have been chosen at this step.

● The default setting is 2 decimal points. You can select from 0 to 15 decimal points by typing the appropriate number.

❸ Press **Enter** and the values in the worksheet are displayed as **,** (Comma) format, rounded to 2 decimal places.

Note: If a range is already formatted, the Worksheet Global command cannot override it. However, a Range Format command can override a Worksheet Global Format command.

FORMAT A RANGE AS CURRENCY

Format ranges B5 to D5, B14 to D14, and B16 to D16 as Currency with thousands separators, and 2 decimal points.

❶ Press **/RFC** (for **R**ange **F**ormat **C**urrency).

❷ Press **Enter** and then type **B5.D5** to select the range.

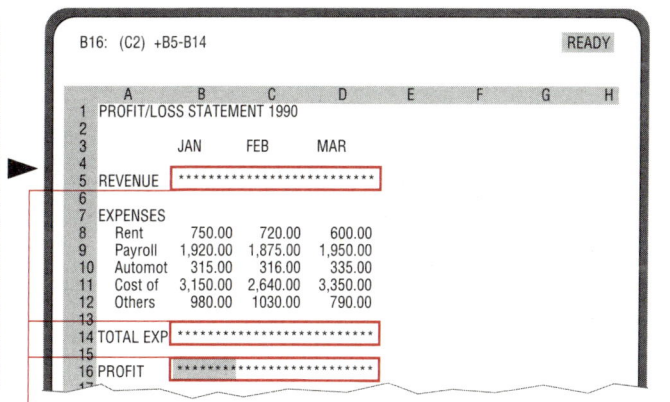

❸ Press **Enter** and all values in the range B5 to D5 are displayed as Currency, rounded to 2 decimal points.

● Asterisks (*) appear because the current format information is too large for the current width of the cells. This problem is corrected on page 41.

❹ Repeat steps **1**, **2** and **3** for ranges B14 to D14 and B16 to D16.

39

CHANGE COLUMN WIDTH

CHANGE THE WIDTH OF ONE COLUMN

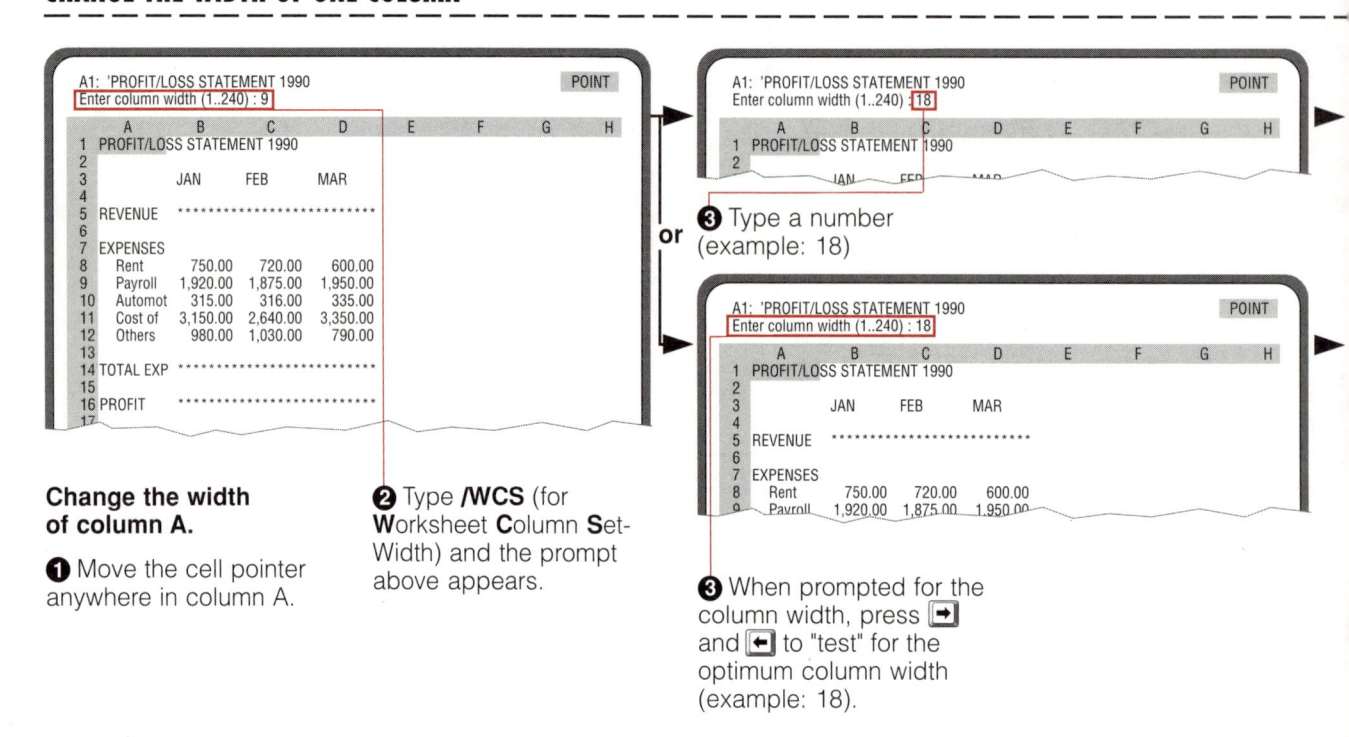

Change the width of column A.

❶ Move the cell pointer anywhere in column A.

❷ Type **/WCS** (for **W**orksheet **C**olumn **S**et-Width) and the prompt above appears.

or

❸ Type a number (example: 18)

❸ When prompted for the column width, press ➡ and ⬅ to "test" for the optimum column width (example: 18).

CHANGE THE WIDTH OF A RANGE OF COLUMNS

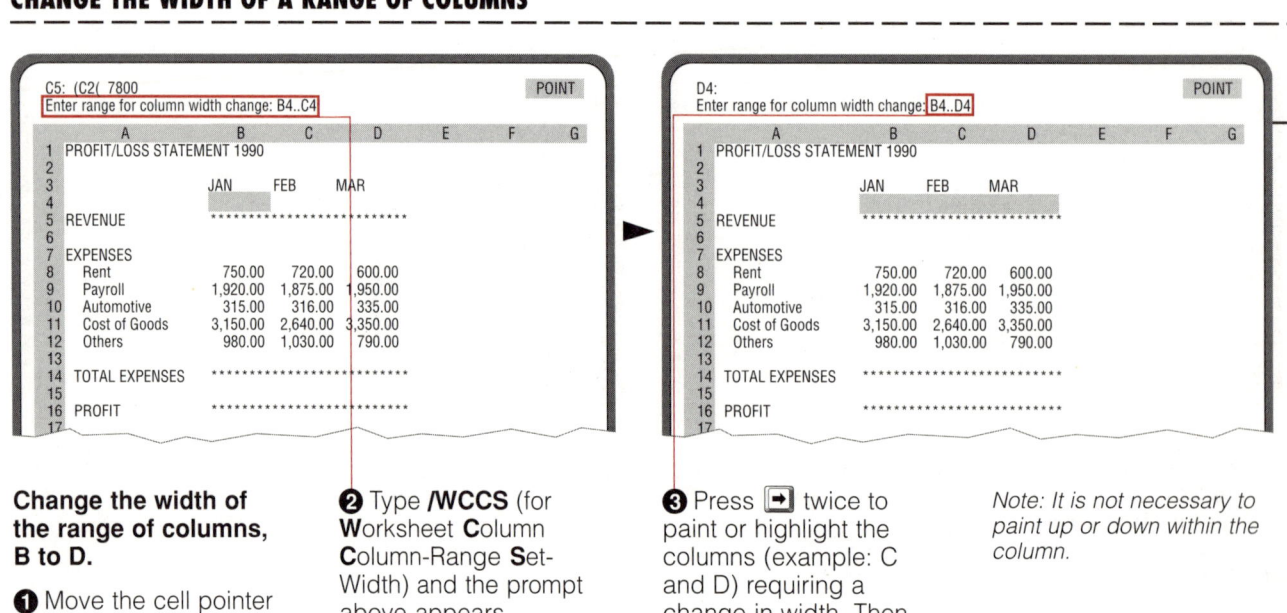

Change the width of the range of columns, B to D.

❶ Move the cell pointer anywhere in column to B (example: B4).

❷ Type **/WCCS** (for **W**orksheet **C**olumn **C**olumn-Range **S**et-Width) and the prompt above appears.

❸ Press ➡ twice to paint or highlight the columns (example: C and D) requiring a change in width. Then press **Enter**.

Note: It is not necessary to paint up or down within the column.

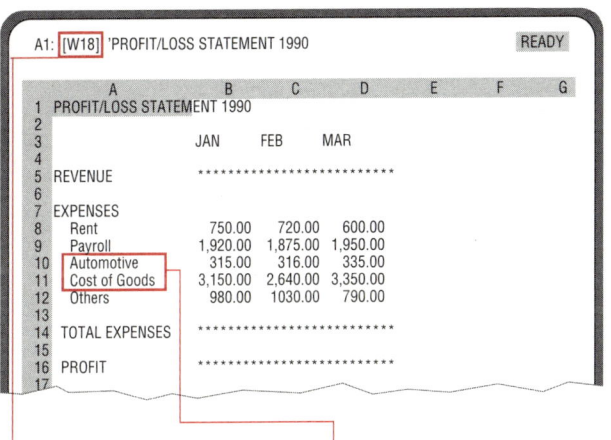

CHANGE CELL FORMAT

CHANGE COLUMN WIDTH

ALIGN LABELS

INSERT/DELETE ROWS OR COLUMNS

CHANGE ALL COLUMN WIDTHS GLOBALLY

❶ Press **/WGC** (For **W**orksheet **G**lobal **C**olumn-Width).

❷ Press ➡ and ⬅ to "test" for the optimal global width or type a number (from 1 to 240) and press **Enter**.

Note: If a column is widened by the worksheet /Worksheet Column Set-width command, the Worksheet Global Column-width command cannot override it.

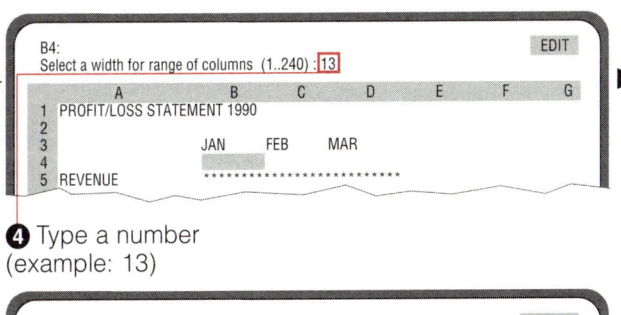

❹ Press **Enter** to accept the new column width setting.

● The column width of A is now wide enough to not truncate long labels such as "Automotive and Cost of Goods".

❹ Type a number (example: 13)

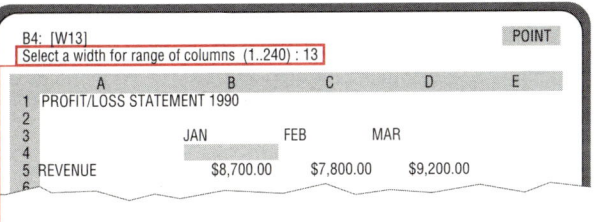

❹ When prompted for the column width, press ➡ and ⬅ to "test" for the optimum column width (example: 13).

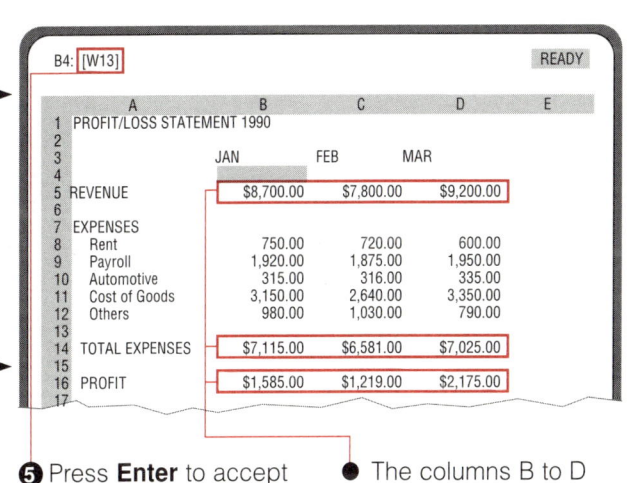

❺ Press **Enter** to accept the new column width settings.

● The columns B to D are now wide enough to display the currency format created on page 39.

CREATE AND EDIT A WORKSHEET

MANAGE YOUR FILES

WORK WITH RANGES

WORK WITH FORMULAS

FORMAT A WORKSHEET

CREATE AND SORT A DATABASE

PRINTING

GRAPHING

HELP

41

ALIGN LABELS

ALIGN LABELS IN RANGES

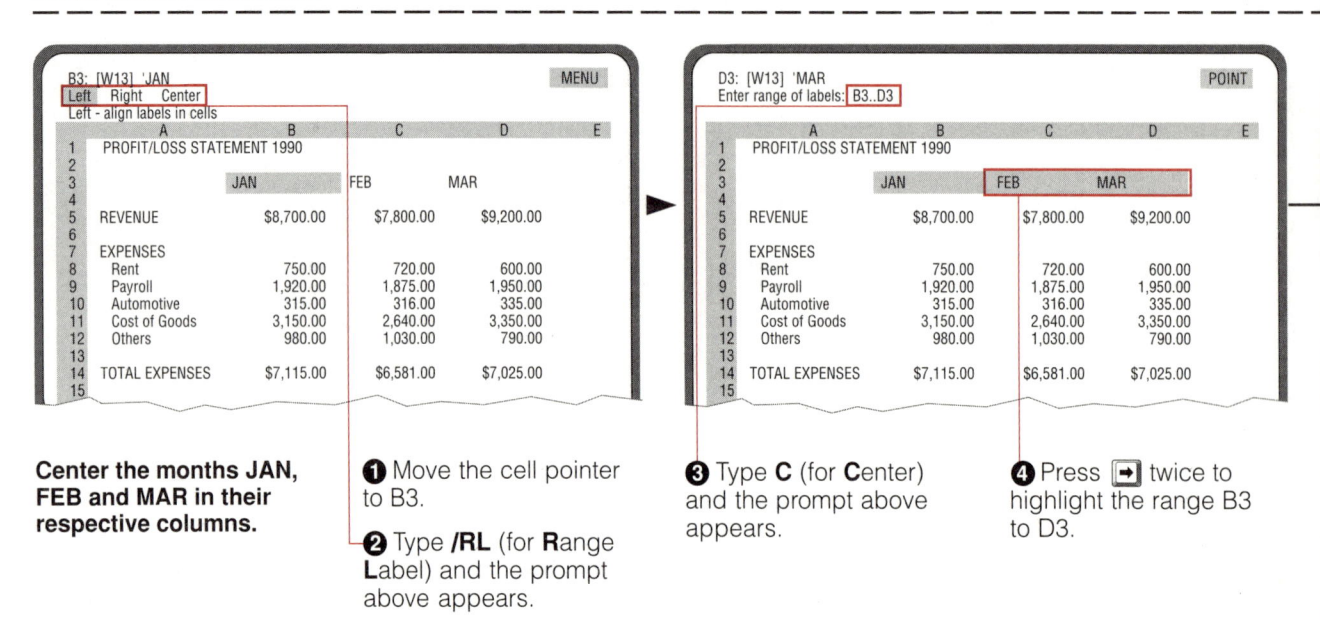

Center the months JAN, FEB and MAR in their respective columns.

① Move the cell pointer to B3.

② Type **/RL** (for **R**ange **L**abel) and the prompt above appears.

③ Type **C** (for **C**enter) and the prompt above appears.

④ Press → twice to highlight the range B3 to D3.

REPEAT LABELS USING THE COPY COMMAND

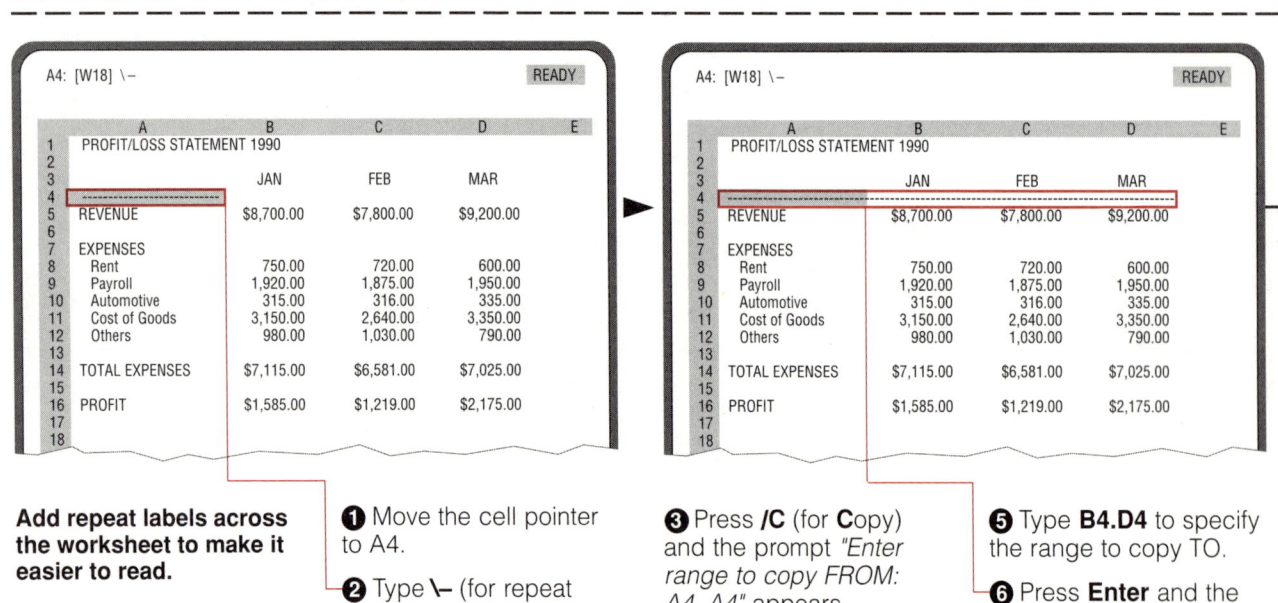

Add repeat labels across the worksheet to make it easier to read.

① Move the cell pointer to A4.

② Type **\\-** (for repeat label) and then press **Enter**.

③ Press **/C** (for **C**opy) and the prompt *"Enter range to copy FROM: A4..A4"* appears.

④ Press **Enter** and the prompt *"Enter range to copy TO: A4"* appears.

⑤ Type **B4.D4** to specify the range to copy TO.

⑥ Press **Enter** and the label is copied to range B4..D4.

| CHANGE CELL FORMAT | CHANGE COLUMN WIDTH | **ALIGN LABELS** | INSERT/DELETE ROWS OR COLUMNS |

```
B3: [W13] ^JAN                                          READY

        A              B          C          D       E
  1  PROFIT/LOSS STATEMENT 1990
  2
  3                   JAN        FEB        MAR
  4
  5  REVENUE       $8,700.00  $7,800.00  $9,200.00
  6
  7  EXPENSES
  8    Rent           750.00     720.00     600.00
  9    Payroll      1,920.00   1,875.00   1,950.00
 10    Automotive     315.00     316.00     335.00
 11    Cost of Goods 3,150.00   2,640.00   3,350.00
 12    Others         980.00   1,030.00     790.00
 13
 14  TOTAL EXPENSES $7,115.00  $6,581.00  $7,025.00
 15
```

❺ Press **Enter** and the months JAN, FEB and MAR are centered in their respective columns.

```
A17: [W18] \-                                           READY

        A              B          C          D       E
  1  PROFIT/LOSS STATEMENT 1990
  2
  3                   JAN        FEB        MAR
  4
  5  REVENUE       $8,700.00  $7,800.00  $9,200.00
  6  ─────────────────────────────────────────────
  7  EXPENSES
  8    Rent           750.00     720.00     600.00
  9    Payroll      1,920.00   1,875.00   1,950.00
 10    Automotive     315.00     316.00     335.00
 11    Cost of Goods 3,150.00   2,640.00   3,350.00
 12    Others         980.00   1,030.00     790.00
 13
 14  TOTAL EXPENSES $7,115.00  $6,581.00  $7,025.00
 15  ─────────────────────────────────────────────
 16  PROFIT        $1,585.00  $1,219.00  $2,175.00
 17  ─────────────────────────────────────────────
 18
```

❼ Move cell pointer to A6 and repeat steps **2** to **6**.

Move cell pointer to A15 and repeat steps **2** to **6**.

Move cell pointer to A17 and repeat steps **2** to **6**.

Note: Remember to change cell numbers to correspond with the row you are copying TO.

CREATE AND EDIT A WORKSHEET

MANAGE YOUR FILES

WORK WITH RANGES

WORK WITH FORMULAS

FORMAT A WORKSHEET

CREATE AND SORT A DATABASE

PRINTING

GRAPHING

HELP

43

INSERT/DELETE ROWS OR COLUMNS

INSERT ROWS

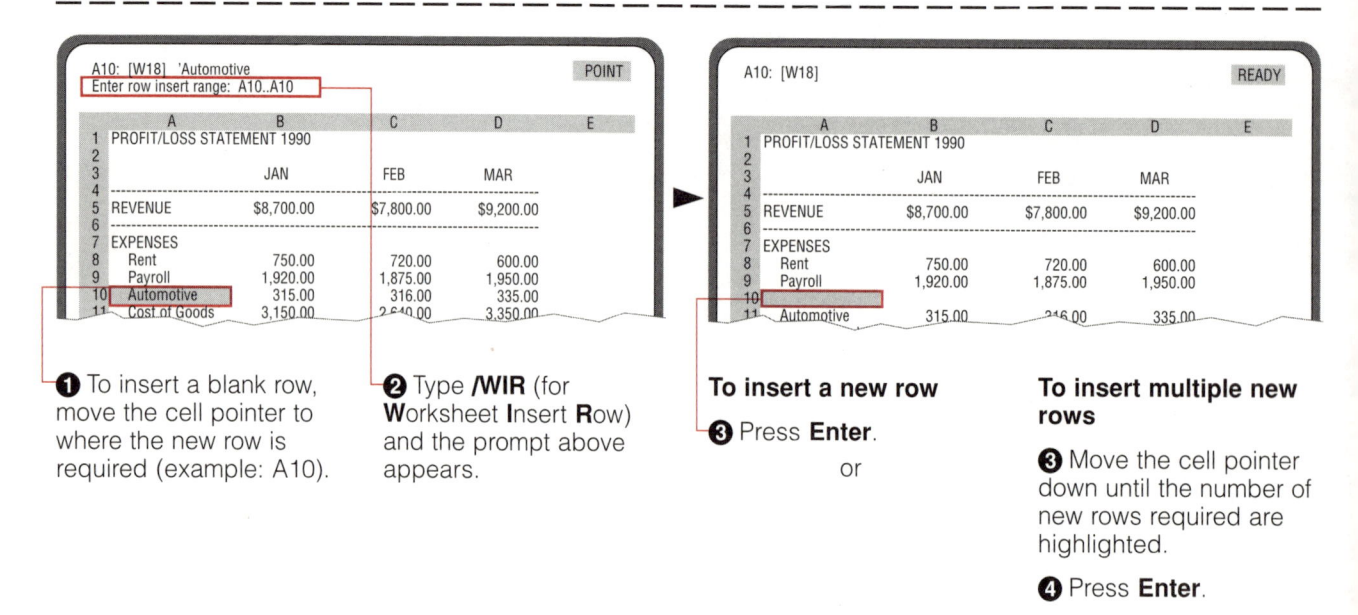

1 To insert a blank row, move the cell pointer to where the new row is required (example: A10).

2 Type **/WIR** (for **W**orksheet **I**nsert **R**ow) and the prompt above appears.

To insert a new row

3 Press **Enter**.

or

To insert multiple new rows

3 Move the cell pointer down until the number of new rows required are highlighted.

4 Press **Enter**.

DELETE ROWS

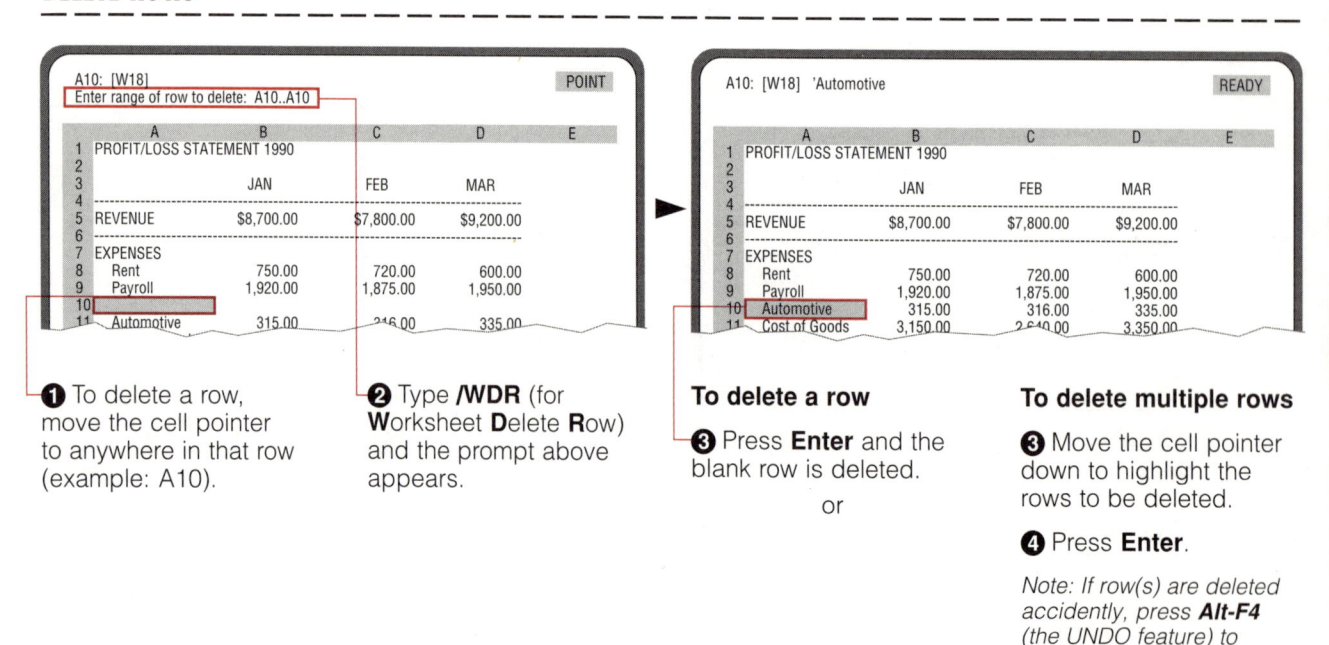

1 To delete a row, move the cell pointer to anywhere in that row (example: A10).

2 Type **/WDR** (for **W**orksheet **D**elete **R**ow) and the prompt above appears.

To delete a row

3 Press **Enter** and the blank row is deleted.

or

To delete multiple rows

3 Move the cell pointer down to highlight the rows to be deleted.

4 Press **Enter**.

Note: If row(s) are deleted accidently, press **Alt-F4** (the UNDO feature) to restore them.

CHANGE CELL FORMAT CHANGE COLUMN WIDTH ALIGN LABELS **INSERT/DELETE ROWS OR COLUMNS**

CREATE AND EDIT A WORKSHEET

INSERT COLUMNS

```
C10: [W13] 316                                    POINT
Enter column insert range: C10..C10
        A              B           C           D           E
1  PROFIT/LOSS STATEMENT 1990
2
3                      JAN         FEB         MAR
4  -----------------------------------------------------
5  REVENUE         $8,700.00   $7,800.00   $9,200.00
6
7  EXPENSES
8    Rent            750.00      720.00      600.00
9    Payroll       1,920.00    1,875.00    1,950.00
10   Automotive     315.00      316.00      335.00
11   Cost of Goods 3,150.00    2,640.00    3,350.00
```

```
C10:                                              READY
Enter column insert range: C10..C10
        A              B           C           D           E
1  PROFIT/LOSS STATEMENT 1990
2
3                      JAN                     FEB         MAR
4  -----------------------------------------------------
5  REVENUE         $8,700.00               $7,800.00   $9,200.00
6
7  EXPENSES
8    Rent            750.00                  720.00      600.00
9    Payroll       1,920.00                1,875.00    1,950.00
10   Automotive     315.00                  316.00      335.00
11   Cost of Goods 3,150.00                2,640.00    3,350.00
```

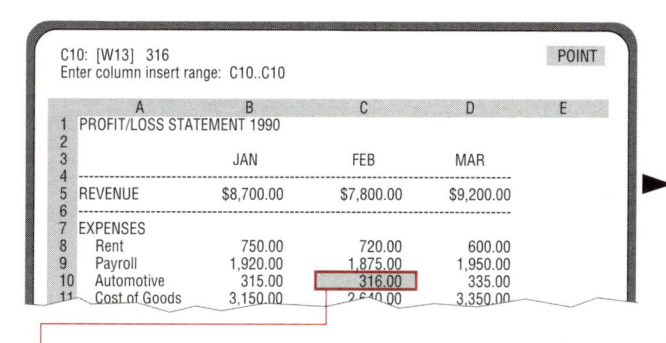

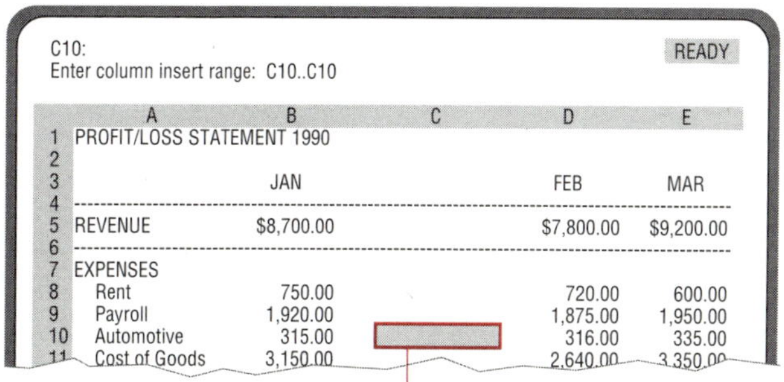

❶ To insert a blank column, move the cell pointer to where the new column is required (example: C10).

❷ Type **/WIC** (for **W**orking **I**nsert **C**olumn) and the prompt above appears.

To insert a new column

❸ Press **Enter**.

or

To insert multiple new columns

❸ Move the cell pointer across until the number of new columns are highlighted.

❹ Press **Enter**.

MANAGE YOUR FILES

WORK WITH RANGES

WORK WITH FORMULAS

FORMAT A WORKSHEET

DELETE COLUMNS

```
C10:                                              POINT
Enter range of columns to delete: C10..C10
        A              B           C           D           E
1  PROFIT/LOSS STATEMENT 1990
2
3                      JAN                     FEB         MAR
4  -----------------------------------------------------
5  REVENUE         $8,700.00               $7,800.00   $9,200.00
6
7  EXPENSES
8    Rent            750.00                  720.00      600.00
9    Payroll       1,920.00                1,875.00    1,950.00
10   Automotive     315.00                  316.00      335.00
11   Cost of Goods 3,150.00                2,640.00    3,350.00
```

```
C10: [W13] 316                                    READY
        A              B           C           D           E
1  PROFIT/LOSS STATEMENT 1990
2
3                      JAN         FEB         MAR
4  -----------------------------------------------------
5  REVENUE         $8,700.00   $7,800.00   $9,200.00
6
7  EXPENSES
8    Rent            750.00      720.00      600.00
9    Payroll       1,920.00    1,875.00    1,950.00
10   Automotive     315.00      316.00      335.00
11   Cost of Goods 3,150.00    2,640.00    3,350.00
```

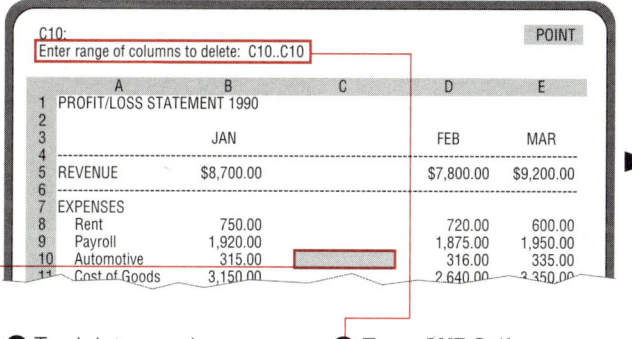

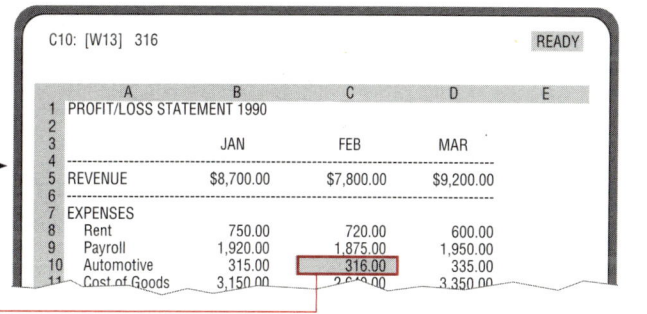

❶ To delete a column, move the cell pointer anywhere in that column (example: C10).

❷ Type **/WDC** (for **W**orksheet **D**elete **C**olumn) and the prompt above appears.

To delete a column

❸ Press **Enter** and the blank column is deleted.

or

To delete multiple columns

❸ Move the cell pointer across to highlight the columns to be deleted.

❹ Press **Enter**.

*Note: If column(s) are deleted accidently, press **Alt-F4** (the UNDO feature) to restore them.*

CREATE AND SORT A DATABASE

PRINTING

GRAPHING

HELP

45

INTRODUCTION

CREATE A DATABASE

A database is a collection of related data in rows and columns in a worksheet.

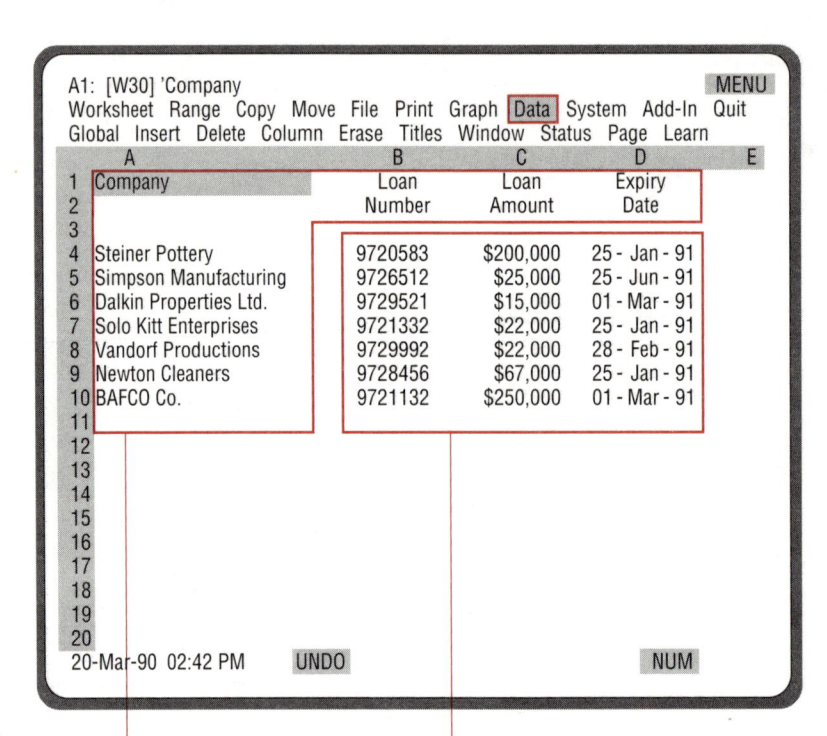

```
A1: [W30] 'Company                                              MENU
Worksheet Range Copy Move File Print Graph Data System Add-In Quit
Global Insert Delete Column Erase Titles Window Status Page Learn
        A                    B          C         D         E
 1  Company                Loan       Loan      Expiry
 2                        Number     Amount      Date
 3
 4  Steiner Pottery        9720583   $200,000  25 - Jan - 91
 5  Simpson Manufacturing  9726512    $25,000  25 - Jun - 91
 6  Dalkin Properties Ltd. 9729521    $15,000  01 - Mar - 91
 7  Solo Kitt Enterprises  9721332    $22,000  25 - Jan - 91
 8  Vandorf Productions    9729992    $22,000  28 - Feb - 91
 9  Newton Cleaners        9728456    $67,000  25 - Jan - 91
10  BAFCO Co.              9721132   $250,000  01 - Mar - 91
11
12
13
14
15
16
17
18
19
20
20-Mar-90  02:42 PM     UNDO                              NUM
```

Note: Always save the database before sorting it. This allows the original database to be retrieved if sorting errors occur.

Create a database using the same skills you have learned from creating a worksheet in 1-2-3.

Before beginning, determine how you will be using your database. Determine if you will be sorting through your client database by name, address, or loan amount. Organize your database accordingly.

● **Enter Labels**

To enter labels, such as company names, refer to page 10 of this guide.

● **Enter Values**

To enter loan numbers, refer to page 12 of this guide.

Note: Since loan numbers are treated as descriptive information and are not used in calculations, they should be entered as labels, not values.

To enter dollar amounts, refer to page 39 of this guide.

To enter dates, refer to page 35 of this guide.

● **Modify Database**

To modify the database (example: adjust column widths, insert/delete column, rows, etc.), refer to page 40 of this guide.

● **Save Database**

When the database is completed, save and name the database. Refer to page 18 of this guide.

INTRODUCTION — SORT A DATABASE

SORT A DATABASE

1-2-3 allows you to sort the items in your database in either ascending or descending order.

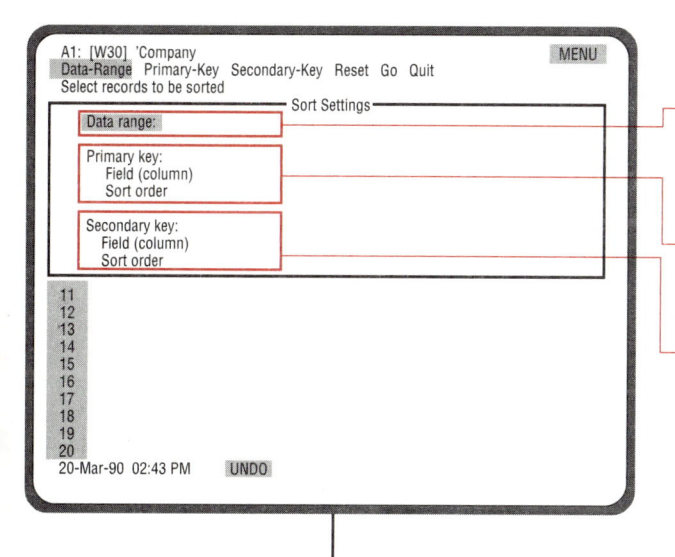

- **Data-Range**
  Specifies the range of the worksheet on which the sort operation will occur.

- **Primary-Key**
  Defines how the information will be sorted.

- **Secondary-Key**
  Defines how the data will be sorted if multiple identical entries appear in the Primary field.

PRIMARY SORT

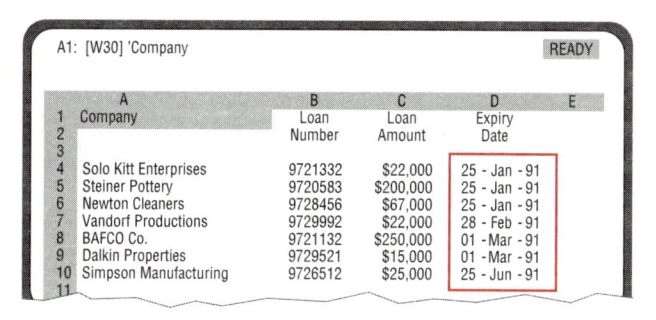

	A	B	C	D
1	Company	Loan Number	Loan Amount	Expiry Date
4	Solo Kitt Enterprises	9721332	$22,000	25 - Jan - 91
5	Steiner Pottery	9720583	$200,000	25 - Jan - 91
6	Newton Cleaners	9728456	$67,000	25 - Jan - 91
7	Vandorf Productions	9729992	$22,000	28 - Feb - 91
8	BAFCO Co.	9721132	$250,000	01 - Mar - 91
9	Dalkin Properties	9729521	$15,000	01 - Mar - 91
10	Simpson Manufacturing	9726512	$25,000	25 - Jun - 91

If: Data-Range = A4..D10
       Primary-Key = D4..D10 (ascending)

Then: 1-2-3 will sort the Expiry Dates (Primary-Key, D4..D10) in ascending order (example: from Jan 91 to Jun 91).

PRIMARY WITH SECONDARY SORT

	A	B	C	D
1	Company	Loan Number	Loan Amount	Expiry Date
4	Newton Cleaners	9728456	$67,000	25 - Jan - 91
5	Solo Kitt Enterprises	9721332	$22,000	25 - Jan - 91
6	Steiner Pottery	9720583	$200,000	25 - Jan - 91
7	Vandorf Productions	9729992	$22,000	28 - Feb - 91
8	BAFCO Co.	9721132	$250,000	01 - Mar - 91
9	Dalkin Properties	9729521	$15,000	01 - Mar - 91
10	Simpson Manufacturing	9726512	$25,000	25 - Jun - 91

If: Data-Range = A4..D10
       Primary-Key = D4..D10 (ascending)
       Secondary-Key = A4..A10 (ascending)

Then: 1-2-3 will sort the two companies from (A4..A10) with similar Expiry Dates in alphabetical order.

CREATE AND EDIT A WORKSHEET

MANAGE YOUR FILES

WORK WITH RANGES

WORK WITH FORMULAS

FORMAT A WORKSHEET

CREATE AND SORT A DATABASE

PRINTING

GRAPHING

HELP

SORT A DATABASE

DEFINE A DATA RANGE

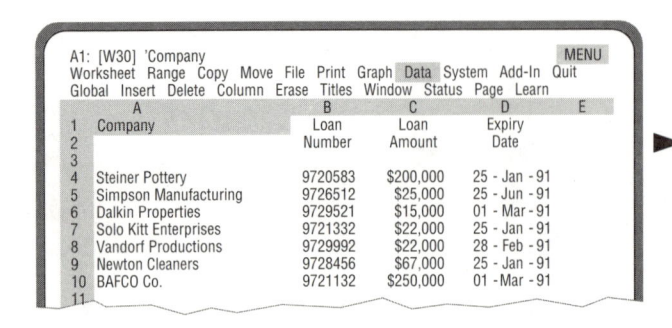

Sort the database by date (Primary-Key) and then by Company (Secondary-Key).

Set up the data range to be sorted.

❶ Type **/DS** (for **D**ata **S**ort) and the screen above appears with Data-Range highlighted.

❷ Press **Enter**.

DEFINE A PRIMARY/SECONDARY SORT

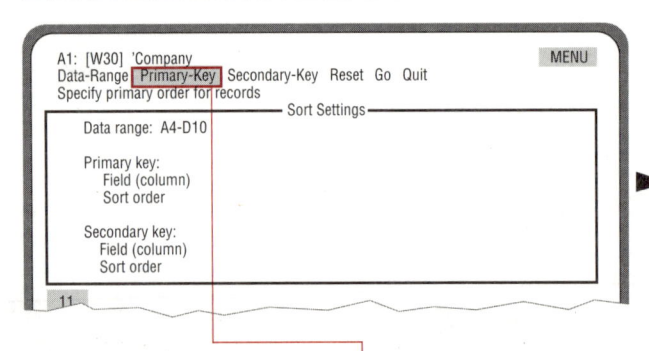

Define the Primary-Key (D4..D4), Secondary-Key (A4..A4) and Sort Order (Ascending or Descending).

❶ Press ➡ to highlight the Primary-Key and then press **Enter**.

❷ Move the cell pointer to a cell in the Primary-Key column (example: D4) and press **Enter**.

● Expiry Date becomes the Primary-Key.

SORT

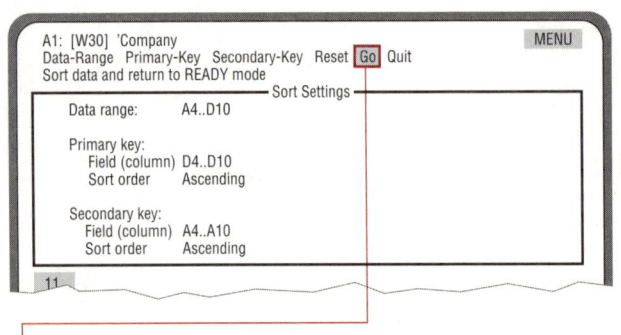

❶ Press ➡ to highlight Go and then press **Enter**.

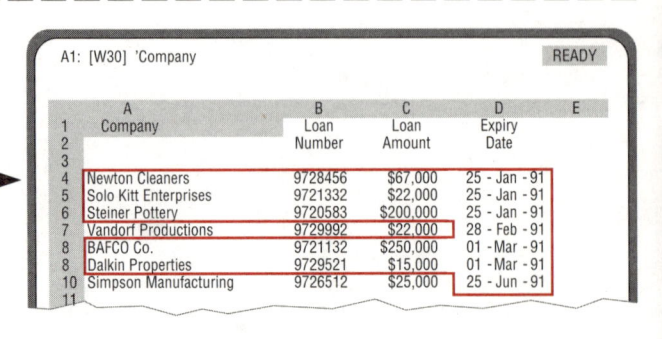

● The screen is sorted as displayed above.

48

INTRODUCTION

SORT A DATABASE

❸ Move the cell pointer to the first cell of the data range (example: A4). Anchor the cell by pressing **.** (period).

❹ Use the arrow keys to move to the last cell of the data range (example: D10) and then press **Enter**.

● The data range is displayed above.

Note: Headings should never be included in the data range, or they will be sorted into the data.

❸ Type **A** (for **A**scending) if you want the data sorted up (example: from A to Z, or from the lowest number/date to the highest number/date).

or

Type **D** (for **D**escending) if you want the data sorted down (example: from Z to A, or from the highest number/date to the lowest number/date.

❹ Press **Enter**. The Primary-Key and Sort Order appears in the dialogue box.

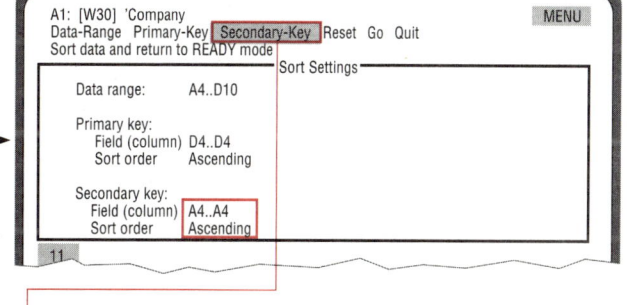

❺ If a Secondary-Key is required, press ➡ to highlight Secondary-Key and then press **Enter**.

● In this example, repeat steps **2**,**3** and **4** using the Secondary-Key column and Sort Order. The Secondary-Key (example: A4) and Sort Order (example: Ascending) is displayed.

Note: If you are satisfied that the database is sorted correctly, the file should be saved (refer to page 18) to make the changes permanent.

49

SELECT A PRINTER

PRINT COMMANDS

```
A1:                                                              MENU
 1    2    3    4
XEROX 4045-50 Courier 10
                              ┌─ Default Settings ─────────────────────┐
Printer:                        Directory: C:\DATA\123DATA
   Interface        Parallel 1
   Auto linefeed    No          Autoexecute macros: Yes
   Margins
      Left 4 Right 76 Top 2 Bottom 2   International:
   Page length    66                Punctuation      A
   Wait           No                   Decimal       Period
   Setup string                        Argument      Comma
   Name           XEROX 4045-50 Couri..  Thousands   Comma
                                    Currency        Prefix: $
Add-In:                             Date format (D4) A (MM/DD/YY)
   1                                Time format (D8) A (HH:MM:SS)
   2                                Negative         Parentheses
   3
   4                                Help access method: Removable
   5                                Clock display:      Standard
   6                                Undo:               Enabled
   7                                Beep:               Yes
   8

20-Mar-90   09:30 AM    UNDO
```

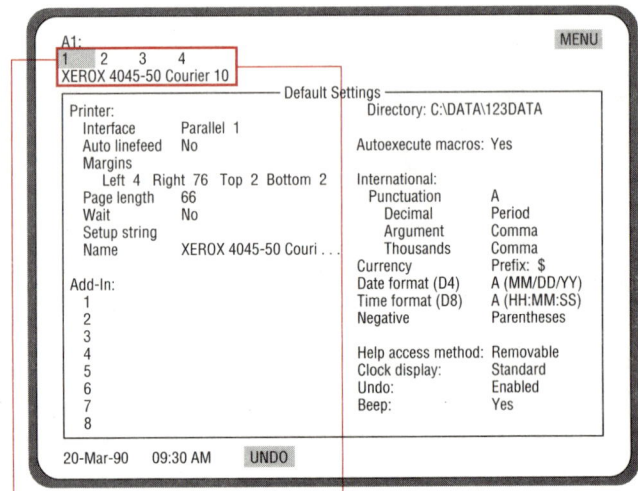

❶ Type **/WGDPN** (for **W**orksheet **G**lobal **D**efault **P**rinter **N**ame) and the screen above appears.

❷ Multiple printer options may be installed. Press → or ← to scan through the printer options. As each option is highlighted, a brief description of the printer is displayed.

❸ Highlight or select the printer you will be using and then press **Enter**.

❹ To select the printer for this session only, type **Q** (for **Q**uit) twice.

or

To install this printer as the default device, type **QUQ** (for **Q**uit **U**pdate **Q**uit).

- Before sending a file to the printer, first check to ensure that the printer you are using is selected by 1-2-3.
- If the required printer is not listed, refer to the Lotus Reference Manual for assistance on using the Install procedure.

Print Screen

Press [Print Screen] to print the entire screen.

Note: This printout captures everything on the screen including the cell and mode indicators, column and row headers and time and date. This screen printout is normally used to aid in the development of a worksheet.

SELECT A PRINTER | **PRINT COMMANDS** | PRINT A REPORT | HEADERS AND FOOTERS

PRINT COMMANDS

- **Range**
  This defines the range or part of the worksheet you want to print.

- **Line**
  Moves the paper in printer up one line.

- **Page**
  Moves the paper in printer to the top of the next page.

- **Options**
  Allows you to create printing settings such as headers, footers, setup strings, etc.

- **Clear**
  Returns the current print setting to the default settings.

- **Align**
  Correctly positions the paper for printing and resets the page number to 1.

- **Go**
  Begins the printing process.

- **Quit**
  Exits this menu and returns 1-2-3 to the ready mode.

```
A1: [W18] 'PROFIT/LOSS STATEMENT 1990                    MENU
Range  Line  Page  Options  Clear  Align  Go  Quit
Specify a range to print
                         ┌─ Print Settings ─┐
Destination:      Printer

Range:

Header:
Footer:

Margins:
  Left 4        Right 76     Top 2    Bottom 2
Borders:
  Columns
  Rows

Setup string:

Page length:      66

Output:           As -Displayed (Formatted)

20-Mar-90  02:42 PM    UNDO                        NUM
```

❶ Type **/PP** (for **P**rint **P**rinter).

- The Print Setting allows you to view all of the settings that apply to the file you are about to print.

CREATE AND EDIT A WORKSHEET

MANAGE YOUR FILES

WORK WITH RANGES

WORK WITH FORMULAS

FORMAT A WORKSHEET

CREATE AND SORT A DATABASE

PRINTING

GRAPHING

HELP

51

PRINT A REPORT

PRINT A REPORT

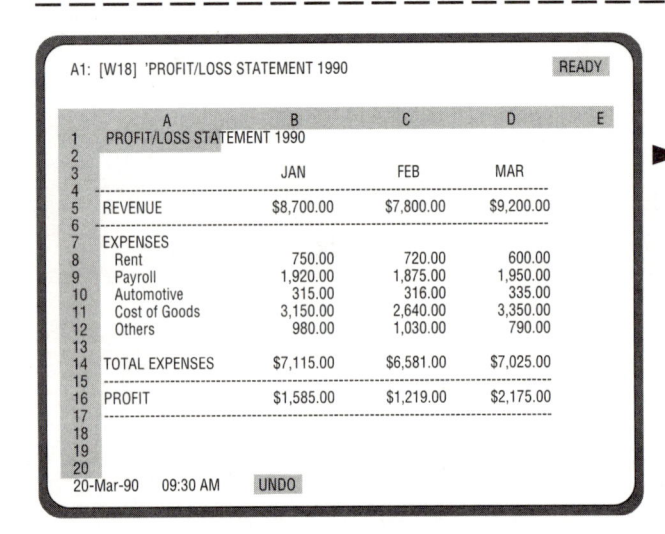

```
A1:  [W18]  'PROFIT/LOSS STATEMENT 1990                          READY
         A              B           C           D         E
  1   PROFIT/LOSS STATEMENT 1990
  2
  3                    JAN         FEB         MAR
  4   ------------------------------------------------
  5   REVENUE        $8,700.00   $7,800.00   $9,200.00
  6   ------------------------------------------------
  7   EXPENSES
  8     Rent             750.00      720.00      600.00
  9     Payroll        1,920.00    1,875.00    1,950.00
 10     Automotive       315.00      316.00      335.00
 11     Cost of Goods  3,150.00    2,640.00    3,350.00
 12     Others           980.00    1,030.00      790.00
 13   ------------------------------------------------
 14   TOTAL EXPENSES  $7,115.00   $6,581.00   $7,025.00
 15   ------------------------------------------------
 16   PROFIT          $1,585.00   $1,219.00   $2,175.00
 17
 18
 19
 20
20-Mar-90  09:30 AM    UNDO
```

Print the worksheet displayed above using 1-2-3's printer default settings.

Note: Make sure the printer you are using has been selected (refer to page 50).

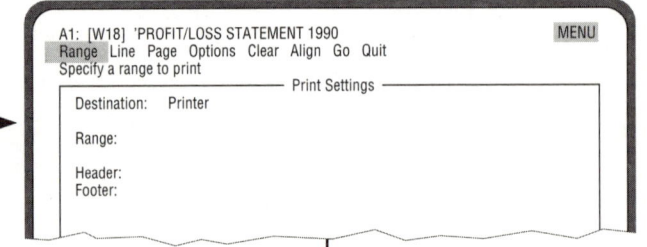

```
A1:  [W18]  'PROFIT/LOSS STATEMENT 1990                          MENU
Range Line Page Options Clear Align Go Quit
Specify a range to print
                              ┌─ Print Settings ─────────────┐
Destination:    Printer       │                              │
                              │                              │
Range:                        │                              │
                              │                              │
Header:                       │                              │
Footer:                       │                              │
```

❶ Type **/PP** (for **P**rint **P**rinter) and the screen above appears.

❷ Type **R** (for **R**ange) and the screen below appears.

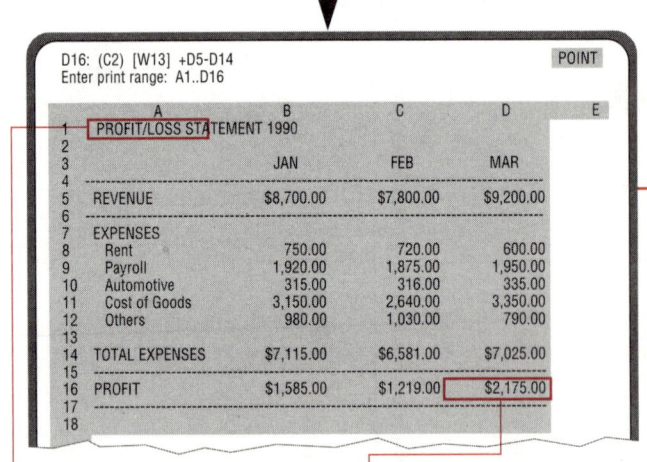

```
D16:  (C2)  [W13]  +D5-D14                                       POINT
Enter print range: A1..D16
         A              B           C           D         E
  1   PROFIT/LOSS STATEMENT 1990
  2
  3                    JAN         FEB         MAR
  4   ------------------------------------------------
  5   REVENUE        $8,700.00   $7,800.00   $9,200.00
  6   ------------------------------------------------
  7   EXPENSES
  8     Rent             750.00      720.00      600.00
  9     Payroll        1,920.00    1,875.00    1,950.00
 10     Automotive       315.00      316.00      335.00
 11     Cost of Goods  3,150.00    2,640.00    3,350.00
 12     Others           980.00    1,030.00      790.00
 13   ------------------------------------------------
 14   TOTAL EXPENSES  $7,115.00   $6,581.00   $7,025.00
 15   ------------------------------------------------
 16   PROFIT          $1,585.00   $1,219.00   $2,175.00
 17
 18
```

❸ Move the cell pointer to the first cell to be printed (example: A1).

❹ Anchor the cell by pressing **.** (period).

❺ Use the arrow keys to move to the last cell to be printed (example: D18).

Note: The Range command is used to define what data is to be printed—even if it is the entire worksheet.

SELECT A PRINTER | PRINT COMMANDS | **PRINT A REPORT** | HEADERS AND FOOTERS

```
A18: [W18]                                              EDIT
Enter setup string:
                        Print Settings
Destination:   Printer
Range:         A1..D18
Header:
Footer:
Margins:
   Left 4      Right 76      Top 2      Bottom 2
Borders:
   Columns
   Rows
Setup string:
Page length:   66
Output:        As-Displayed (Formatted)

20-Mar-90    09:50 AM
```

```
            PROFIT/LOSS STATEMENT 1990
                        JAN         FEB         MAR
REVENUE               $8,700.00   $7,800.00   $9,200.00
EXPENSES
   Rent                  750.00      720.00      600.00
   Payroll             1,920.00    1,875.00    1,950.00
   Automotive            315.00      316.00      335.00
   Cost of Goods       3,150.00    2,640.00    3,350.00
   Others                980.00    1,030.00      790.00
TOTAL EXPENSES        $7,115.00   $6,581.00   $7,025.00
PROFIT                $1,585.00   $1,219.00   $2,175.00
```

❻ Press **Enter** and the range A1..D18 is displayed above.

❼ Type **OS** (for **O**ptions **S**etup) and the prompt above appears.

❽ Type the setup string required (examples below) and then press **Enter**. Then type **Q** (for **Q**uit) to return to the main print menu.

Note: If no setup string is typed, the printer's default setting is used.

❾ To start the printing process type **AG** (for **A**lign **G**o).

*Note: To stop the printing process, press **Ctrl-Break**.*

Setup String Examples

Xerox Laser Printer	Portrait, Top Drawer	\0272\027c1\027m4200,0,0,0,4200
	Portrait, Middle Drawer	\0272\027c2\027m4200,0,0,0,4200
	Portrait, Bottom Drawer	\0272\027c3\027m4200,0,0,0,4200
IBM Proprinter and Quietwriter	5 Pitch	\027\087\001
	10 Pitch	\018
	12 Pitch	\027\058
Epson Dot Matrix Printer	10 Pitch	\027\080
	12 Pitch	\027\077
	15 Pitch	\027\103
	8 Lines per inch	\027\048
	6 Lines per inch	\027\050

Setup strings send a series of commands to the printer to make the worksheet print properly.

HINTS FOR CONTINUOUS FORM FEED PRINTERS

To move the paper in the printer up one line

Type **/PPL** (for **P**rint **P**rinter **L**ine).

To advance the paper to the top of the next page

Type **/PPP** (for **P**rint **P**rinter **P**age).

CREATE AND EDIT A WORKSHEET

MANAGE YOUR FILES

WORK WITH RANGES

WORK WITH FORMULAS

FORMAT A WORKSHEET

CREATE AND SORT A DATABASE

PRINTING

GRAPHING

HELP

53

HEADERS AND FOOTERS

ADD A HEADER AND FOOTER

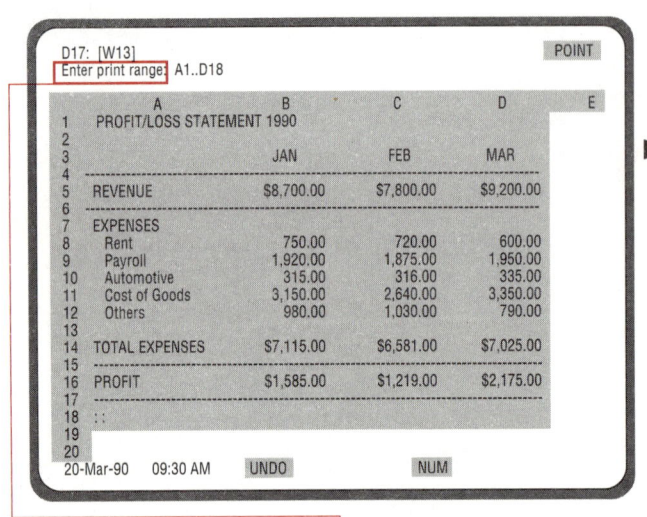

A header is text that appears at the top of each printed page of the worksheet.

A footer is text that appears at the bottom of each printed page of the worksheet.

Note: Headers and footers are handled the same way and can contain up to three areas of text.

Add a header and footer to the worksheet PROFIT/LOSS STATEMENT 1990.

❶ Type **/PPR** (for **P**rint **P**rinter **R**ange) and the prompt above appears.

❷ Move the cell pointer to A1 and then type **.** (period) to anchor the cell.

❸ Press ➡ until the print range A1..D18 is painted.

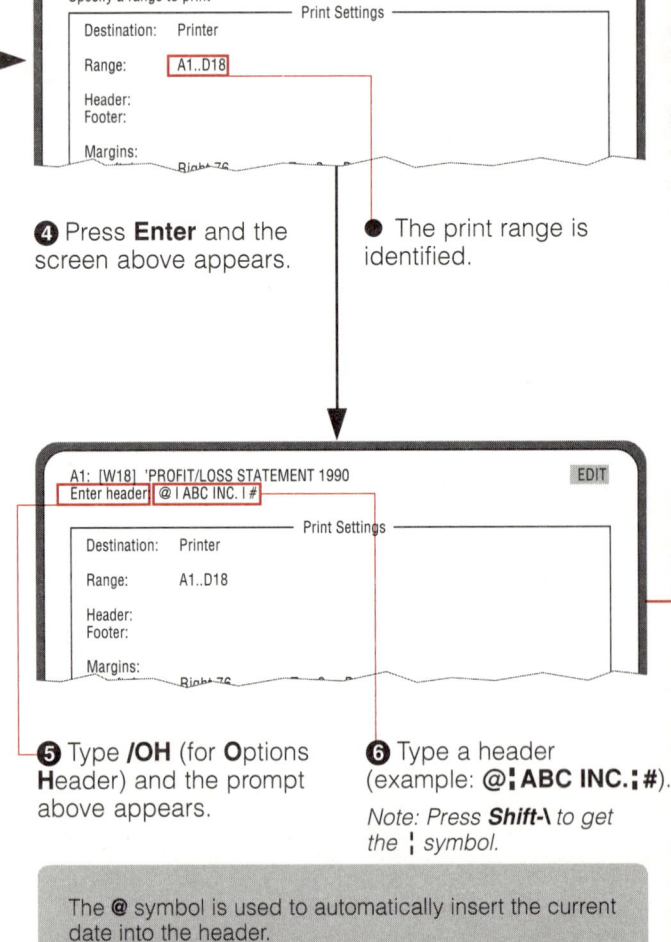

❹ Press **Enter** and the screen above appears.

● The print range is identified.

❺ Type **/OH** (for **O**ptions **H**eader) and the prompt above appears.

❻ Type a header (example: **@¦ABC INC.¦#**).

*Note: Press **Shift-** to get the ¦ symbol.*

The **@** symbol is used to automatically insert the current date into the header.

ABC.INC is the second item in the header.

The **#** symbol is used to automatically number the printed pages, beginning with 1.

The ¦ symbol separates the three items in a header.

Text without a ¦ symbol to its left is left justified.

Text with a ¦ symbol to its left is centered.

Text with a ¦¦ symbol to its left is right justified.

| SELECT A PRINTER | PRINT COMMANDS | PRINT A REPORT | **HEADERS AND FOOTERS** |

```
A1: [W18] 'PROFIT/LOSS STATEMENT 1990                    MENU
 Header  Footer  Margins  Borders  Setup  Pg-Length  Other  Quit
Create a header
┌─────────────────── Print Settings ───────────────────
│ Destination:   Printer
│
│ Range:         A1..D18
│
│ Header:        @ | ABC INC. | #
│ Footer:
│
│ Margins:
                 Right 76
```

7 Press **Enter** and the screen above appears.

● The header to print is identified.

```
A1: [W18] 'PROFIT/LOSS STATEMENT 1990                    MENU
 Header  Footer  Margins  Borders  Setup  Pg-Length  Other  Quit
Create a footer
┌─────────────────── Print Settings ───────────────────
│ Destination:   Printer
│
│ Range:         A1..D18
│
│ Header:        @ | ABC INC. | #
│ Footer:        | CONSOLIDATED STATEMENTS
│
│ Margins:
                 Right 76
```

10 Press **Enter** and the screen above appears.

● The footer to print is identified.

11 Type **Q** (for **Q**uit) and then **AG** (for **A**lign **G**o) to print the worksheet.

```
A1: [W18] 'PROFIT/LOSS STATEMENT 1990                    EDIT
Enter footer  CONSOLIDATED STATEMENTS
┌─────────────────── Print Settings ───────────────────
│ Destination:   Printer
│
│ Range:         A1..D18
│
│ Header:        @ | ABC INC. | #
│ Footer:
│
│ Margins:
                 Right 76
```

8 Type **F** (for **F**ooter) and the prompt above appears.

9 Type a footer (example: CONSOLIDATED STATEMENTS).

*Note: When using a footer, a **/WP** (for **W**orksheet **P**age) symbol **::** must be inserted after the last line of the worksheet in **Column A** to ensure the footer prints on every page.*

*The cell containing the **::** symbol **must** be included in the print range.*

To clear all print settings

From the READY mode type **/PPCA** (for **P**aper **P**rinter **C**lear **A**ll).

```
20-Mar-90              ABC INC.                          1

PROFIT/LOSS STATEMENT 1990
                        JAN         FEB         MAR
─────────────────────────────────────────────────────
REVENUE              $8,700.00   $7,800.00   $9,200.00

EXPENSES
  Rent                  750.00      720.00      600.00
  Payroll             1,920.00    1,875.00    1,950.00
  Automotive            315.00      316.00      335.00
  Cost of Goods       3,150.00    2,640.00    3,350.00
  Others                980.00    1,030.00      790.00

TOTAL EXPENSES       $7,115.00   $6,581.00   $7,025.00
─────────────────────────────────────────────────────
PROFIT               $1,585.00   $1,219.00   $2,175.00
─────────────────────────────────────────────────────




                 CONSOLIDATED STATEMENTS
```

CREATE AND EDIT A WORKSHEET

MANAGE YOUR FILES

WORK WITH RANGES

WORK WITH FORMULAS

FORMAT A WORKSHEET

CREATE AND SORT A DATABASE

PRINTING

GRAPHING

HELP

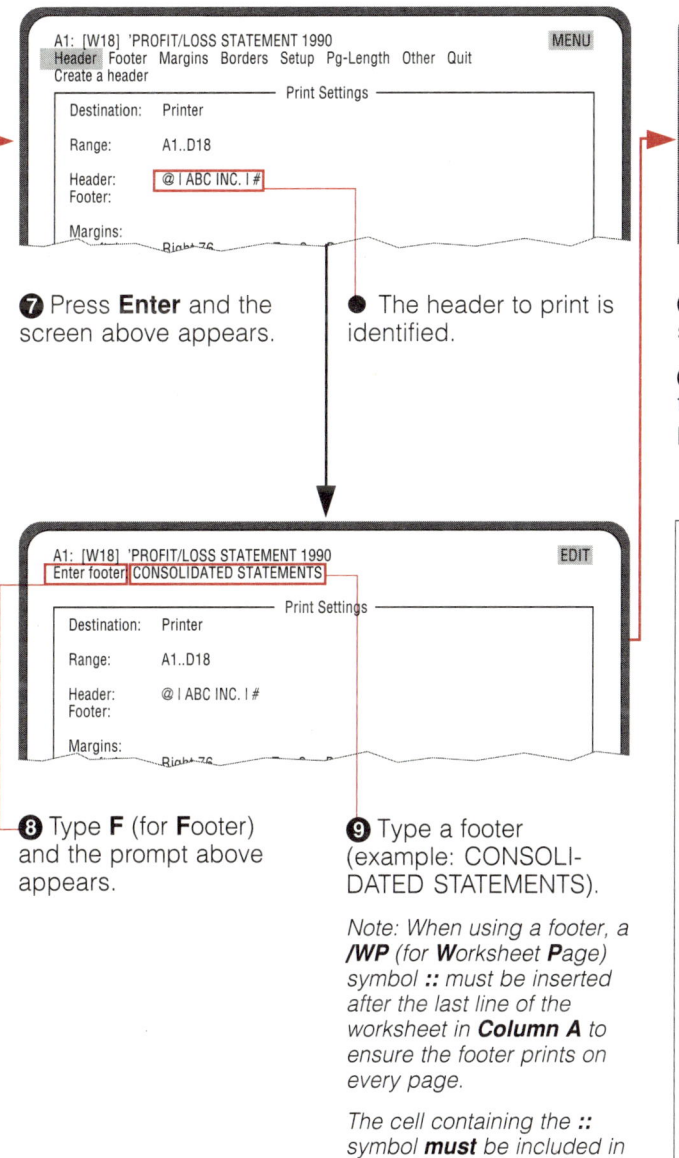

DEFINE TYPE OF GRAPH   **IDENTIFY DATA RANGES**

DEFINE TYPE OF GRAPH

```
A5: [W18] 'REVENUE                                           READY

             A              B          C          D          E
 1   PROFIT/LOSS STATEMENT 1990
 2
 3                         JAN        FEB        MAR        APR
 4   ----------------------------------------------------------
 5   REVENUE            $8,700.00  $7,800.00  $9,200.00  $10,575.00
 6
 7   EXPENSES
 8     Rent               750.00     720.00     600.00     $550.00
 9     Payroll          1,920.00   1,875.00   1,950.00   $1,950.00
10     Automotive         315.00     316.00     335.00     $220.00
11     Cost of Goods    3,150.00   2,640.00   3,350.00   $1,900.00
12     Others             980.00   1,030.00     790.00     $315.00
13
14   TOTAL EXPENSES    $7,115.00  $6,581.00  $7,025.00  $4,935.00
15
16   PROFIT            $1,585.00  $1,219.00  $2,175.00  $5,640.00
17
18
19
20
20-Mar-90  08:07 PM       UNDO                    NUM
```

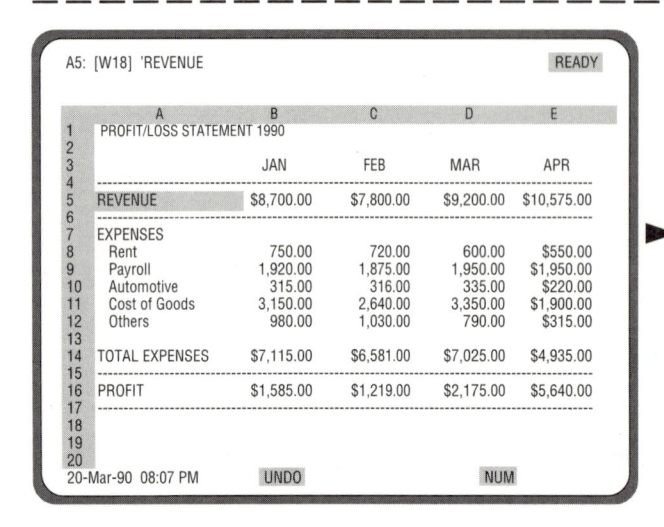

```
A5: [W18] 'REVENUE                                           MENU
Line  Bar  XY  Stack-Bar  Pie
Bar graph
                                         ┌── Graph Settings ──
Type: Line                   Titles:  First
                                      Second
X:                                    X axis
A:                                    Y axis
B:
C:                                                 Y scale:     X scale:
D:                                      Scaling    Automatic    Automatic
E:                                      Lower
F:                                      Upper
                                        Format     (G)          (G)
Grid: None      Color: No               Indicator  Yes          Yes

     Legend:          Format:           Data labels:     Skip: 1
A    revenue
B                     Both
C                     Both
D                     Both
E                     Both
F                     Both
20-Mar-90  09:05 PM                                      NUM
```

Create a bar graph of REVENUE, TOTAL EXPENSES and PROFIT for the months JAN to APR.

❶ Type **/G** (for **G**raph) to access the Graph Settings screen.

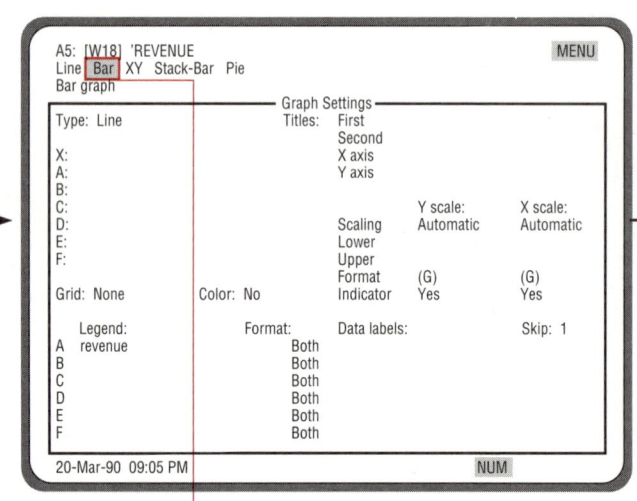

❷ Type **T** (for **T**ype of graph).

❸ Select the type of graph (example: Press ➡ once to select the Bar graph) and then press **Enter**.

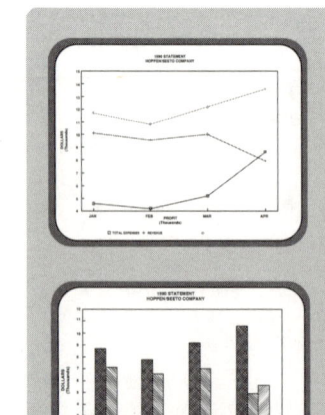

Line Graph
Visually displays the change in data against time. Used for projections and to identify trends.

Bar Graph
Visually displays two or more data items against time. Also used for projections and to identify trends.

Bar Stack
Visually displays the proportion each data item represents with respect to each other.

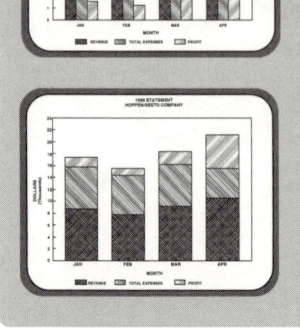

Note: XY and Pie graphs may also be created in 1-2-3.

IDENTIFY DATA RANGES

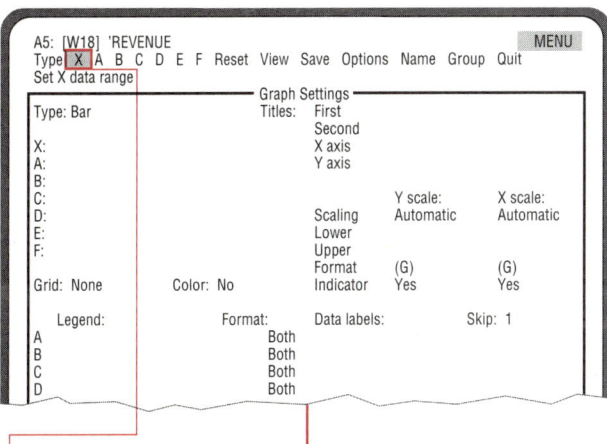

```
A5: [W18] 'REVENUE                                          MENU
Type X A B C D E F Reset View Save Options Name Group Quit
Set X data range
                         ┌─ Graph Settings ─────────────────┐
Type: Bar                │ Titles:  First                   │
                         │          Second                  │
X:                       │          X axis                  │
A:                       │          Y axis                  │
B:                       │                                  │
C:                       │                  Y scale:   X scale:
D:                       │ Scaling          Automatic  Automatic
E:                       │ Lower                            │
F:                       │ Upper                            │
                         │ Format           (G)        (G)  │
Grid: None  Color: No    │ Indicator        Yes        Yes  │
                         │                                  │
    Legend:   Format:    │ Data labels:                Skip: 1
A                         Both
B                         Both
C                         Both
D                         Both
```

❹ Press ➡ once to select the X data range. Then press **Enter**.

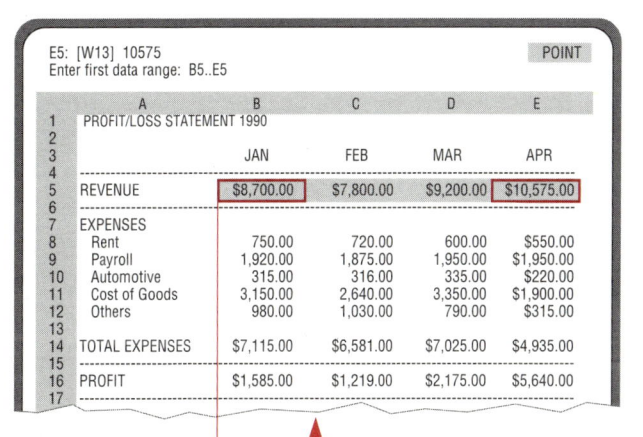

```
E5: [W13] 10575                                             POINT
Enter first data range: B5..E5
       A              B          C          D          E
  1  PROFIT/LOSS STATEMENT 1990
  2
  3                  JAN        FEB        MAR        APR
  4  ─────────────────────────────────────────────────────
  5  REVENUE       $8,700.00  $7,800.00  $9,200.00  $10,575.00
  6
  7  EXPENSES
  8    Rent           750.00     720.00     600.00    $550.00
  9    Payroll      1,920.00   1,875.00   1,950.00  $1,950.00
 10    Automotive     315.00     316.00     335.00    $220.00
 11    Cost of Goods 3,150.00   2,640.00   3,350.00  $1,900.00
 12    Others         980.00   1,030.00     790.00    $315.00
 13  ─────────────────────────────────────────────────────
 14  TOTAL EXPENSES $7,115.00  $6,581.00  $7,025.00  $4,935.00
 15
 16  PROFIT        $1,585.00  $1,219.00  $2,175.00  $5,640.00
 17
```

❾ Move the cell pointer to B5 (the start of the Revenue range) and paint the range B5..E5.

❿ Repeat steps **8** and **9** to define ranges B (TOTAL EXPENSES) and C (PROFIT).

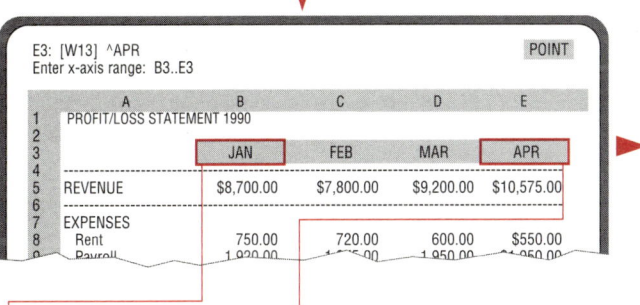

```
E3: [W13] ^APR                                              POINT
Enter x-axis range: B3..E3
       A              B          C          D          E
  1  PROFIT/LOSS STATEMENT 1990
  2
  3                  JAN        FEB        MAR        APR
  4  ─────────────────────────────────────────────────────
  5  REVENUE       $8,700.00  $7,800.00  $9,200.00  $10,575.00
  6
  7  EXPENSES
  8    Rent           750.00     720.00     600.00    $550.00
```

❺ Move the cell pointer to the first cell that you want to appear on the X axis of the graph. (example: JAN).

❻ Press **.** (period) to anchor the range.

❼ Press ➡ four times to move to the last cell of the X data range (example: E3) and then press **Enter**.

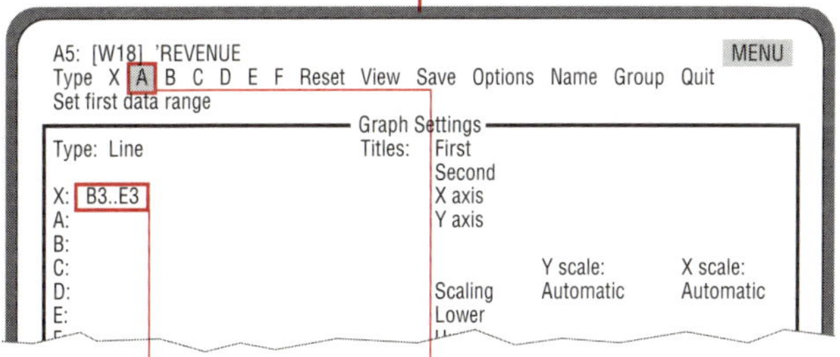

```
A5: [W18] 'REVENUE                                          MENU
Type X A B C D E F Reset View Save Options Name Group Quit
Set first data range
                         ┌─ Graph Settings ─────────────────┐
Type: Line               │ Titles:  First                   │
                         │          Second                  │
X: B3..E3                │          X axis                  │
A:                       │          Y axis                  │
B:                       │                                  │
C:                       │                  Y scale:   X scale:
D:                       │ Scaling          Automatic  Automatic
E:                       │ Lower                            │
```

● The X data range is displayed above.

❽ Press ➡ to move to A, (first range of data cell to be plotted on your graph) and press **Enter**.

*Note: Data ranges A through F will appear on the **vertical axis** of your graph.*

To reset graph settings

Type **/GR**, and follow the prompts.

57

CREATE LEGEND/TITLES

VIEW A GRAPH

CREATE A LEGEND

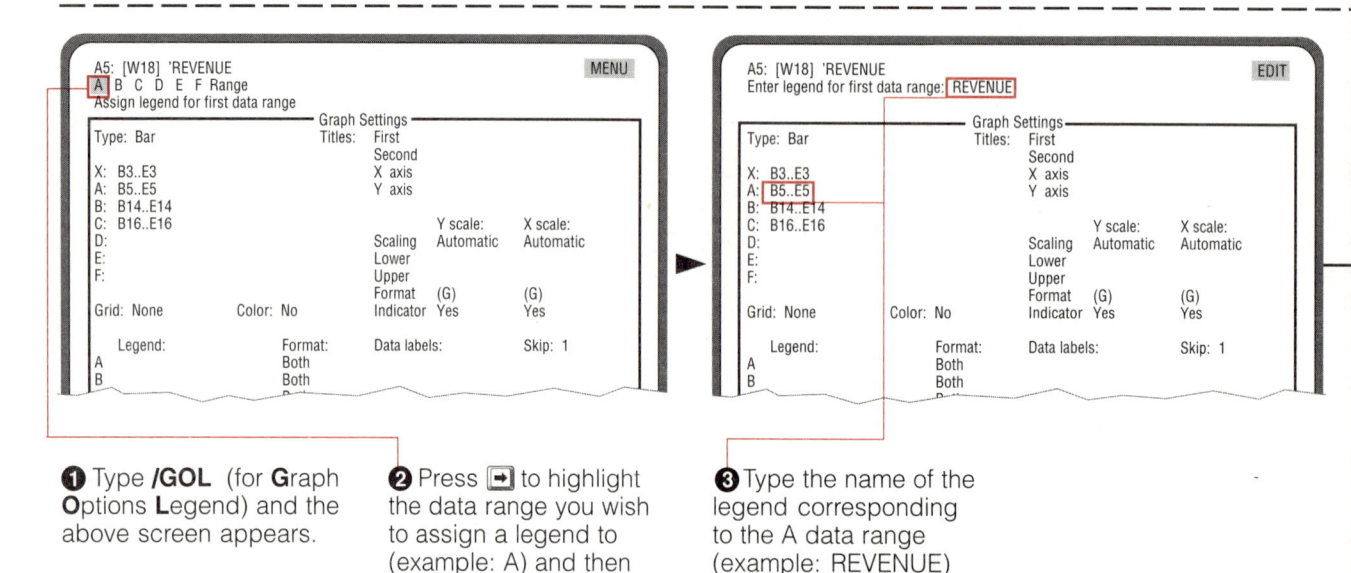

❶ Type **/GOL** (for **G**raph **O**ptions **L**egend) and the above screen appears.

❷ Press ➡ to highlight the data range you wish to assign a legend to (example: A) and then press **Enter**.

❸ Type the name of the legend corresponding to the A data range (example: REVENUE) and then press **Enter**.

CREATE TITLES

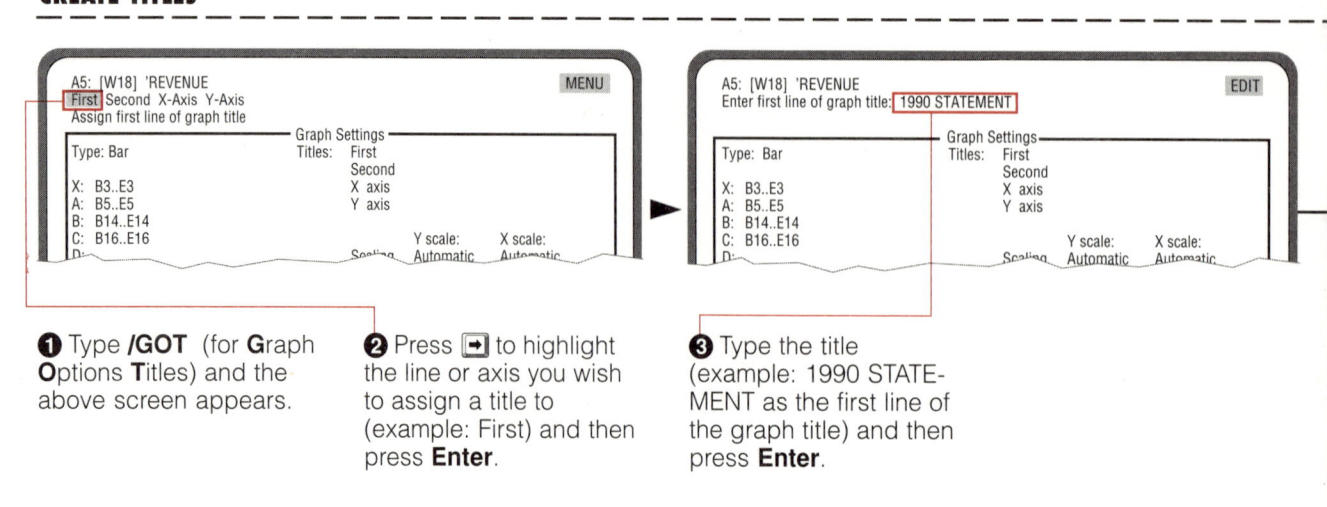

❶ Type **/GOT** (for **G**raph **O**ptions **T**itles) and the above screen appears.

❷ Press ➡ to highlight the line or axis you wish to assign a title to (example: First) and then press **Enter**.

❸ Type the title (example: 1990 STATEMENT as the first line of the graph title) and then press **Enter**.

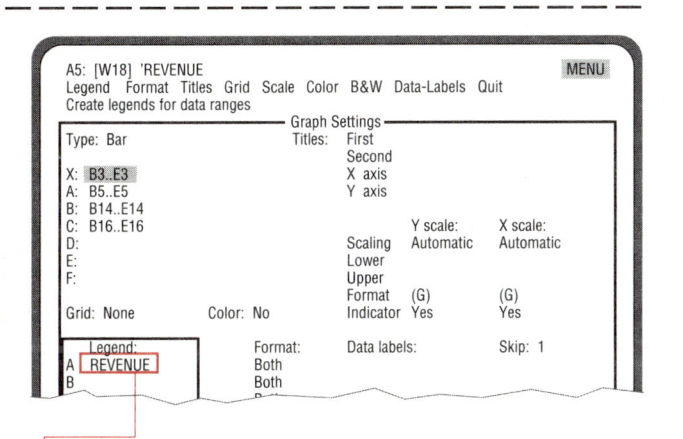

DEFINE TYPE OF GRAPH   IDENTIFY DATA RANGES   **CREATE LEGEND/TITLES**   **VIEW A GRAPH**

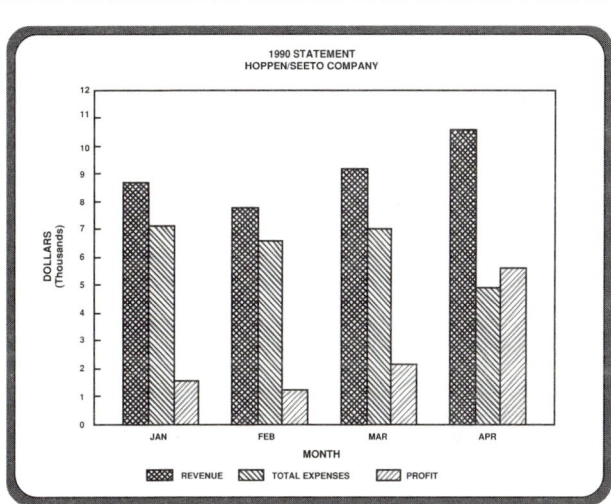

VIEW A GRAPH

```
A5: [W18] 'REVENUE                                    MENU
Legend Format Titles Grid Scale Color B&W Data-Labels Quit
Create legends for data ranges
                        ┌── Graph Settings ──────────────────┐
Type: Bar               │ Titles:   First                    │
                        │           Second                   │
X:  B3..E3              │           X axis                   │
A:  B5..E5              │           Y axis                   │
B:  B14..E14            │                                    │
C:  B16..E16            │                    Y scale:   X scale:
D:                      │ Scaling            Automatic  Automatic
E:                      │ Lower                              │
F:                      │ Upper                              │
                        │ Format             (G)        (G)  │
Grid: None  Color: No   │ Indicator          Yes        Yes  │
            Legend:     │ Format:   Data labels:        Skip: 1
A  REVENUE              │ Both
B                       │ Both
```

● The legend name appears above.

❹ Repeat steps **2** and **3** for all legend titles.

❶ Type **/GV** (for **G**raph **V**iew) and the Bar graph is displayed above.

❷ Press **Esc** to return to the Graph Settings dialogue box.

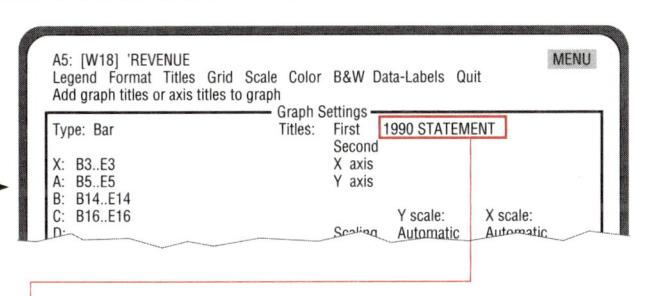

```
A5: [W18] 'REVENUE                                    MENU
Legend Format Titles Grid Scale Color B&W Data-Labels Quit
Add graph titles or axis titles to graph
                        ┌── Graph Settings ──────────────────┐
Type: Bar               │ Titles:   First    1990 STATEMENT  │
                        │           Second                   │
X:  B3..E3              │           X axis                   │
A:  B5..E5              │           Y axis                   │
B:  B14..E14            │                                    │
C:  B16..E16            │                    Y scale:   X scale:
D:                      │ Scaling            Automatic  Automatic
```

● The title appears above.

❹ Repeat steps **2** and **3** to complete the titles for the Second line of the graph title, the horizontal X-axis and the vertical Y-axis.

NAME A GRAPH

To save a graph with its worksheet, type **/GNC** (for **G**raph **N**ame **C**reate). Type the graph title (up to 15 characters) and then press **Enter**.

To view the graph again, type **/GNU** (for **G**raph **N**ame **U**se), highlight the graph name, and press **Enter**.

PRINT A GRAPH

To print a graph using PrintGraph, it must first be saved in PIC format. For more details on printing graphs, refer to your Lotus Reference Manual.

CREATE AND EDIT A WORKSHEET

MANAGE YOUR FILES

WORK WITH RANGES

WORK WITH FORMULAS

FORMAT A WORKSHEET

CREATE AND SORT A DATABASE

PRINTING

GRAPHING

HELP

59

HELP

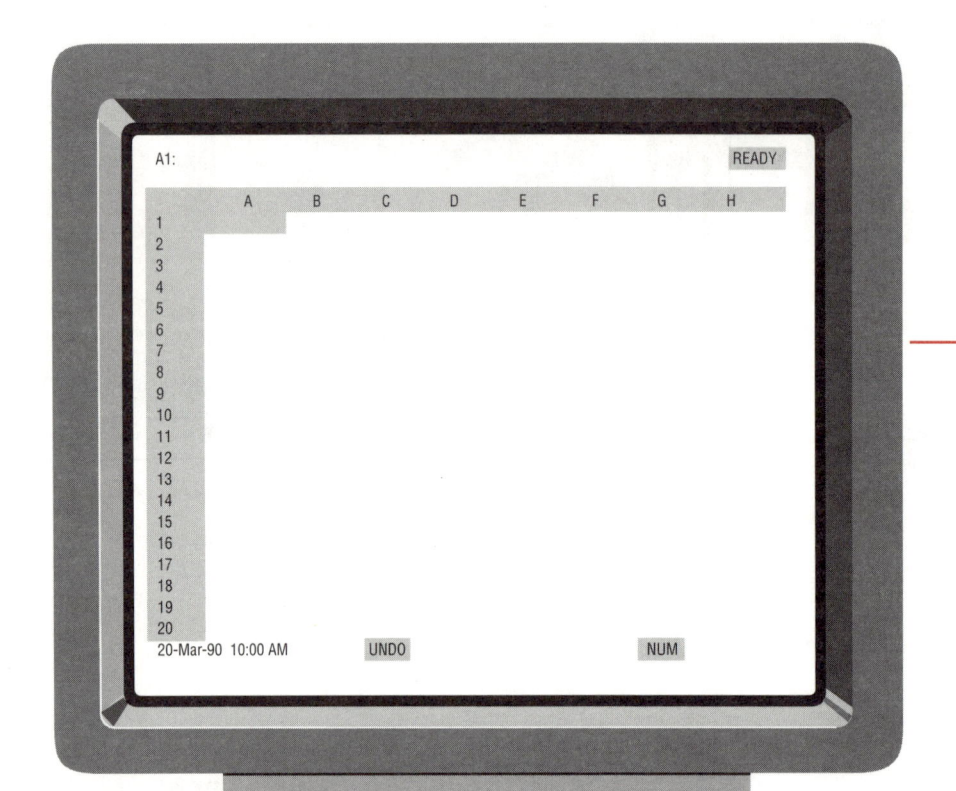

❶ Press **F1** to access the Help Index screen.

Note: When 1-2-3 displays an error message, press **F1** to get Help to correct the error.

To cancel the error message, press **Esc**.

❷ From this screen, you can get progressively more detailed Help on any of the topics listed.

To select any topic on the screen, use the arrow keys ➡, ⬆, ⬅, ⬇.

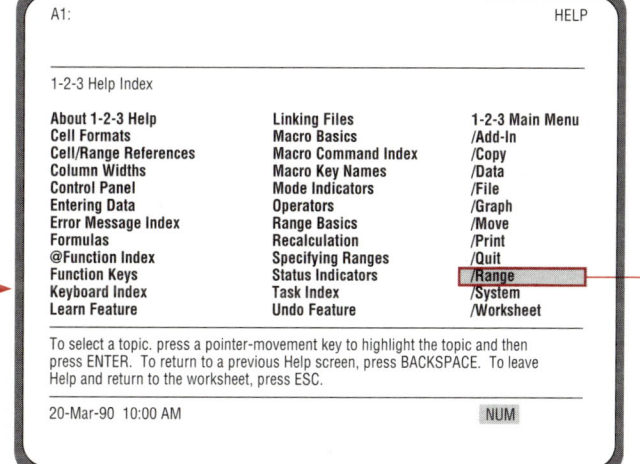

```
A1:                                                              HELP

1-2-3 Help Index

About 1-2-3 Help        Linking Files           1-2-3 Main Menu
Cell Formats            Macro Basics            /Add-In
Cell/Range References   Macro Command Index     /Copy
Column Widths           Macro Key Names         /Data
Control Panel           Mode Indicators         /File
Entering Data           Operators               /Graph
Error Message Index     Range Basics            /Move
Formulas                Recalculation           /Print
@Function Index         Specifying Ranges       /Quit
Function Keys           Status Indicators       /Range
Keyboard Index          Task Index              /System
Learn Feature           Undo Feature            /Worksheet

To select a topic, press a pointer-movement key to highlight the topic and then
press ENTER.  To return to a previous Help screen, press BACKSPACE.  To leave
Help and return to the worksheet, press ESC.

20-Mar-90  10:00 AM                                       NUM
```

❸ Press **Enter** to display information on the selected topic.

*Note: To return to the worksheet, press **Esc**.*

CONTEXT SENSITIVE HELP (F1)

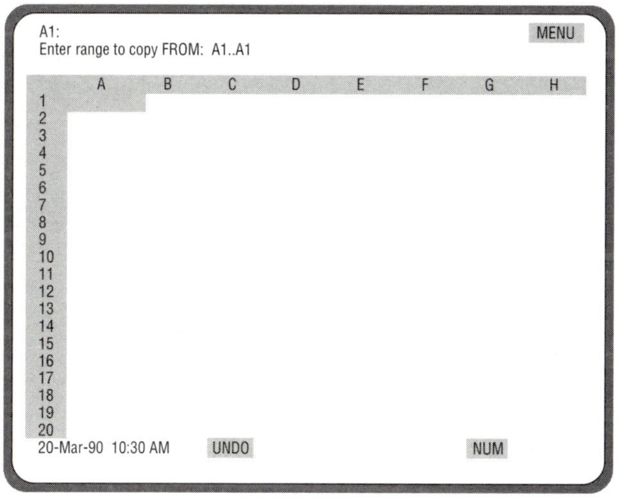

```
A1:                                                              MENU
Enter range to copy FROM: A1..A1

       A      B      C      D      E      F      G      H
  1
  2
  3
  ...
 20
20-Mar-90  10:30 AM         UNDO                          NUM
```

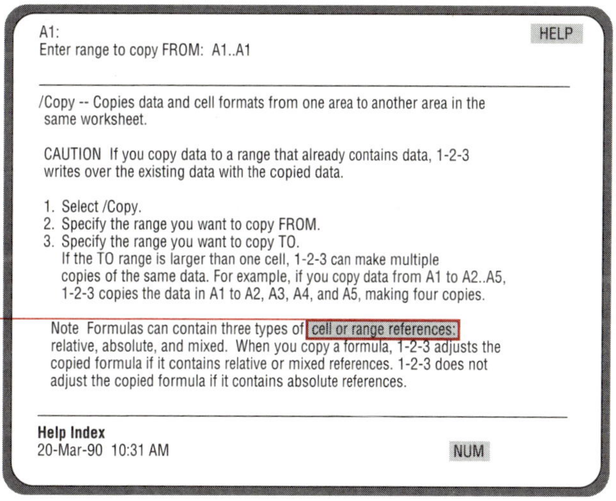

```
A1:                                                              HELP
Enter range to copy FROM: A1..A1

/Copy -- Copies data and cell formats from one area to another area in the
same worksheet.

   CAUTION  If you copy data to a range that already contains data, 1-2-3
   writes over the existing data with the copied data.

   1. Select /Copy.
   2. Specify the range you want to copy FROM.
   3. Specify the range you want to copy TO.
      If the TO range is larger than one cell, 1-2-3 can make multiple
      copies of the same data.  For example, if you copy data from A1 to A2..A5,
      1-2-3 copies the data in A1 to A2, A3, A4, and A5, making four copies.

   Note  Formulas can contain three types of cell or range references:
   relative, absolute, and mixed.  When you copy a formula, 1-2-3 adjusts the
   copied formula if it contains relative or mixed references. 1-2-3 does not
   adjust the copied formula if it contains absolute references.

Help Index
20-Mar-90  10:31 AM                                       NUM
```

❶ After issuing a command (example: **/C** (for **C**opy), press **F1** and the next screen appears.

❷ The cell range references are highlighted. Press **Enter** to get more information on this subject.

or

Press ⬇ and then **Enter** to return to the Help Index screen.

61

Index

Page

COLUMNS
- Delete 45
- Format 40, 41, 45
- Insert 45
- Width 40, 41

COMMANDS
- Select Commands 8, 9
- Print Commands 51

CURSOR MOVEMENT KEYS
- Backspace 11
- Delete 11
- End 11
- Home 11
- Right/Left Arrows 11
- Shift-Tab 11
- Tab 11

DATABASE
- Create 46
- Primary Sort 47-49
- Secondary Sort 47-49

DIRECTORIES
- Create 15
- Default Directories 16, 17
- Organization 14
- Post 1,2,3,4 14
- Root 14

EXIT 3

FILE
- Display 17
- Naming 15

FORMAT
- Change Cell Format 38, 39
- Columns 40, 41, 45
- Currency 38, 39
- Date 38
- Fixed 38
- General 38
- Labels 42, 43
- Percent 38
- Rows 44
- , (Comma) 38

Page

FORMULAS
- Absolute Cell References 36, 37
- Order of Precedence 33
- Relative Cell References 36, 37
- @Functions 34, 35

GRAPHING
- Identify Data Ranges 57
- Legend 58, 59
- Name 59
- Print 59
- Reset Graph Settings 57
- Titles 58, 59
- Type 56
- View 59

HELP 60, 61

INSTALL 3

LABELS
- Align 42, 43
- Correct/Edit 10, 11
- Entering 10, 11
- Prefixes 10, 11
- Repeat Labels 42, 43

NAVIGATION 6, 7

PRINTING
- Graphs 59
- Headers and Footers 54, 55
- Print Commands 51
- Print Report 52, 53
- Print Screen 50
- PrintGraph 3, 59
- Select Printer 50

RANGES
- Anchor 26, 27
- Copy 24-27
- Erase 28, 29
- Find String 31
- Move 28, 29
- Paint 26, 27
- Replace String 31
- Select 23, 26, 27
- Search 30

Page

ROWS
- Delete 44
- Insert 44

SAVE 18

TRANSLATE 3, 59

UNDO 29, 44, 45

VALUES
- Automatic Recalculation 12, 13
- Entering a Formula 12, 13
- Entering Numbers 12, 13

WORKSHEET
- Cell 4
- Cell Address 5
- Cell Entry 5
- Cell Format 5
- Cell Width 5
- Erase 8, 9, 20, 21
- Format 38-45
- Retrieve 20, 21
- Save 18

@FUNCTIONS
- @AVG 34
- @DATE 34, 35
- @MAX 34
- @MIN 34
- @ROUND 34
- @SUM 34, 35